The

LAND

of

FAITH

ii

© 2021 by Denise S. Millben

Published by Lord's Image Publishing
P.O. Box 1945
Muncie, IN 47308
www.lordsimage.com

Paperback published 2021

Cover by Tashema Davis & Lord's Image

ISBN 978-0-9984160-2-1

Printed in the United States States of America

Contents

PREFACE

The purpose of this book is to enlighten and inspire believers to not only walk in faith, but to choose to live in The Land of Faith.

The primary scripture that supports this statement is Hebrews 11:6, "But without faith it is impossible to please Him, for he who comes to God must believe that He is, and that He is a rewarder of those who diligently seek Him."

I would like you to explore The Land of Faith with me. The Land of Faith is not heaven, the new Jerusalem, or paradise. My description of The Land of Faith may challenge your belief system and stimulate your spiritual development. The Land of Faith is based on how you think and what you chose to believe deep in your heart. It is where your soul dwells. It is how you release your faith to believe all that the scriptures have said. The Land of Faith is in the Kingdom of God. That is why the word of God is directing people to this influential and undisputable Kingdom. It is where grace, peace, direction and development occur. This is where answers to prayer reside.

A few years ago, I was motivated by the Lord to teach about The Land of Faith. As I began to speak, I realized that there was more to this topic than I could exhaust on in one discourse. My husband graciously allowed me several weeks to complete the series with no thought of it evolving into a book at the time. Then I felt the stirring of the Holy Spirit to begin to pull the sermons together and create a book on the subject. Why? Because, unfortunately, many believers do not live in faith. They used the faith they have been given to become a child of God, (that is saving faith) but many do not take that faith past salvation unless some major problem occurs in their family or in their physical wellbeing. This faith, that God has given every man, woman, boy and girl is given to them to profit within a specific realm.

What I believe God is telling us is that we can live in this world, but not be of this world. We can walk among people and be involved in daily activities as others, but the real activity we are engaged in is in the realm of faith.

This book is going to reveal to you the place where the Lord wants his children to live. He wants to give them instructions as to how they should conduct themselves once they have decided to live there.

Hope Thou In God

Why are you cast down, O my soul?
And why are you disquieted within me?
Hope in God; For I shall yet praise Him,
The help of my countenance and my God.
Psalm 45:5 (KJV)

HOPE IS A FEELING of wanting something to happen and thinking that it could occur; a feeling that something good will come true, someone or something may be able to provide help: someone or something that gives you a reason for hoping or an expectation and desire for a certain thing to materialize. A feeling of trust.[1]

Be of good courage,
And He shall strengthen your heart,
all you who hope in the Lord
(Psa. 31:24 KJV).

What I see in these passages is an admonishment given to believers to HOPE. I call HOPE the rocket booster to your faith. It all begins with hope, but you cannot stay there. As you can see, even in these scriptures, the word says to Hope but then you must do something. Hoping is the beginning to this new way of living. Hope is the jumper cable to the faith battery. You jump start your faith with hope.

Proverbs 13:12 says,

"Hope deferred makes the heart sick,
but when the desire comes, *it is* a tree of life."

Hope takes us to the threshold of The Land of Faith, but then it is up to us to travel further into the unknown or pitch our tents up and down the bank of Hope without ever tapping into all that the Father has in store for us. Praise helps escort you into this new realm. The Psalmist says, "I will praise thee, O Lord my God with my heart...." (Psa. 86:12 KJV). That is one thing that you can begin to do. Praise the Lord!

Hope says, "this is what I believe is coming to me", but praise takes it a step further and says, "I will praise Him for the work being done even if I don't see it thus far."

During the height of the Space Shuttle Program there were many challenges to overcome and one of these challenges was funds to continue research needed to make the space shuttles reusable. The rocket boosters were the first solid fuel engines to be used for primary propulsion on space vehicles. The spaceship needed to have extra thrust during the first two minutes of flight. These external fuel tanks are a pair of giant rockets with a single, two-minute purpose: to get the shuttle, it's cargo and the crew off the launch pad and into the air. Immediately following the ignition of the shuttles' main engines the boosters are fired; the shuttle then leaps off the launch pad in a dramatic and heart stopping display of pyrotechnics. The boosters push the shuttle to speeds of more than 3,000 miles per hour. Once the boosters have pushed the rocket past the earth's atmosphere, they are detonated from the rocket, and the primary engines take complete control of the shuttle.[2]

Can you see how hope could be understood through this analogy?

You have a desire, a dream, a belief that is burning inside your heart. The hope is that these things will come to pass. You want it to happen. You have not seen it, no one told you that they are about to give it to you, or take you to where it is, or anything. You just hope this will transpire. Without hope your faith rocket will not be able to get past the earth's atmosphere. The earth's atmosphere is filled with fear, unbelief, worry, questions and negative words, not only from others, but sometimes from within your own mind. All these elements latch on to your faith and make it difficult to lift off because of the weight. So, without the rocket booster it won't get off the launching pad.

Hope is something that comes from God to ignite the engine of your faith and to assist you in lift off. Hope is that extra thrust you need to get past the doubt, worry and fear.

Every great person began their journey with hope. They might have merely seen something that prompted them to desire a change. Or they might have been involved with something that needed to change because the old was no longer working. Hope begins with a desire to see something different. I believe that all inventors begin their quest for an invention with hope. As we look at some outstanding people and trace their lives before they became famous, we will find hope intricately woven throughout their lives.

Dr. Martin Luther King was propelled by hope. You can hear it in just about every speech he presented. He hoped that one day his children would be considered and treated equal to white children and that all people would respect and judge each other for their character and not by their skin color. Hope was his rocket booster and then he had to put his faith to work.

President John F. Kennedy was a man that had hope. The hope to see a change in the United States of America. Then he had to put that hope to work to convince his countrymen that putting a man on the moon and bringing equality for all people were realistic and significant goals for our nation.

Anna Connelly was the first woman to invent the fire escape. How could she have done this back in 1887? Or Maria Beasley who saw the disasters at sea and, hoping that no one else would die from such disasters, she invented the life raft. These women had hope even though women were underrepresented and their rights ignored. Women did not even gain the right to vote until 1920! Hope propelled these women into a male dominated arena, but they did not allow that to hinder them. Hope was their rocket boosters. Then they began to do something about it.

Is doing something going to be easy? Absolutely not, but that doesn't matter. Hope is the impetus you need to accomplish the task at hand.

How can a person change their lives from a gangster to a saint? Ask David Wilkerson who had hope that the neighborhoods in New York could change, but he knew that it could only be changed by changing people. Rev. David Wilkerson shared the true story of hope in a community during his first five years in New York where he ministered to disillusioned youth. Or, in other words, youth without hope. He gave these youth hope. Because of that hope he offered, many young people turned from drugs, gangs, violence and became followers of Jesus Christ. One young man was Nicky Cruz whose life was radically changed. Hope brought him to Jesus who, in turn transformed his life. David Wilkerson wrote about this ministry, in the book *The Cross and the Switch Blade*[3]. This book sold 16 million copies and became a movie viewed by an estimated 50 million people. Though this book is 55 years old, the message still brings hope. I encourage you to read this amazing testimony of how hope pushed a juvenile delinquent out of the street life full of drugs, violence and pain, into a life of faith and praise to God. Hope helped pull him out of the atmosphere of the streets into the atmosphere of faith. That is when everything changed.

Hope is the thing that the street evangelist offered to broken and hurting people. A promise that something can change their lives forever for the good. Once hope is received and embraced, faith kicks in and massive changes are seen in people's lives. The gospel will do that for people. What we must offer is hope. These testimonies are the rocket boosters to people's mustard seed rocket of faith.

Nihilism is defined as a state of hopelessness;[4] this is where many people are living. Hope on the other hand is confident expectation or anticipation. It is not mere wishful thinking. Today II Corinthians 4:4 is truer than ever, "in whom the God of this world hath blinded the minds of them who believe not, lest the light of the glorious gospel of Christ, who is the image of God, should shine unto them."

The god of this world, who has many names including Lucifer, Bealzibub and most commonly Satan, has used many tactics to blind the minds of people. One of them is nihilism. The frightening result is a numbing detachment from others and a self-destructive disposition toward the world. Life without meaning, hope and love breeds a dark hearted, mean-spirited, outlook that destroys individuals.

I believe that nihilism is a philosophy that has a spirit attached to it. Currently that spirit is so prevalent in every culture, that many in underdeveloped nations fail to plan for their lives because they lack confidence in their future. Wait! we don't have to go around the world to third world countries to observe that spirit working at the core of people's hearts. There are several pockets located across the United States that are existing in that hopelessness. They do not see any way out of their personal dilemma. They have not seen anyone in their sphere of influence get out, so they feel that no one can get out. Therefore, they are destined to die without hope. They consequently turn to a wild and destructive lifestyle.

The enemy of our soul's strategy is to keep the gospel message from being preached, declared, announced, or proclaimed because the gospel gives hope. If by chance the gospel does get to people, the enemy tries to snatch it out of their hearts before it can take root. The worthless ideologies of man's invention, (even if they seem valuable), cannot produce the hope needed in this hour to counterattack the pervasive attitude of hopelessness.

The enemy's strategy is to bombard us through the media with endless displays of hopelessness in different communities around the world. The fear of unclean air, chemtrails, water pollution, food shortages, viruses, COVID, threats of attacks from locally and abroad, global warming, government failings and shutdowns and the list goes on and on. This is designed to fill the hearts of people with all kinds of negative information so that when they hear the gospel, it is hard to receive because they are so full of all the other negative news.

The god of this world has blinded the minds of people who do not believe. Oftentimes, we do not realize that all it takes is a little bit of hope to boost people into the atmosphere of faith and a confident expectation that God is going to do just what He promised.

The Bible states in Ephesians 2:12:

That at that time ye were without Christ,
being aliens from the commonwealth of Israel,
and strangers from the covenants of promise,
having no hope, and without God in the world.

HIS PROMISES

Nihilism is no hope, no light, no direction, no plan, No God.

However, Jesus came "that we might have life and that more abundantly" (John 10:10). Hope is waiting with expectation.

The One problem is that some people miss out because they are too focused on looking and waiting for things God never said, but they need to zero in on what He promised.

He promised to give us grace in the time of need.
He promised never to leave us nor forsake us.
He promised that the Comforter would come and lead and guide us.
He promised to keep us in perfect peace if we keep our minds stayed on Him (Isa. 26:3).
He promised that even if we are cast down we will not be destroyed (II Cor. 4:8).

He told us in II Cor. 4:8-9 that we would be "... troubled on every side, but not distressed; perplexed, but not forsaken; struck down, but not destroyed." I stand today as a witness to the faithfulness of the Almighty God. He has kept His word!

By entering through faith into what God has always wanted to do for us - set us right with Him, make us fit for Him - we have it all together with God because of our Master Jesus. And that's not all: We throw open our doors to God and discover at the same moment that he has already thrown open his door to us. We find ourselves standing where we always hoped we might stand, out in the wide-open spaces of God's grace and glory, standing tall and shouting our praise.

There's more to come: We continue to shout our praise even when we're hemmed in with troubles, because we know how troubles can develop passionate patience in us, and how that patience in turn forges the tempered steel of virtue, keeping us alert for whatever God will do next. In alert expectancy, such as this, we're never left feeling shortchanged. Quite the contrary - we can't round up enough containers to hold everything God generously pours into our lives through the Holy Spirit (Romans 5:1-5 MESSAGE).

By far the main objective are expectant waiting or hope, is God, His word, His judgment, and His mercy.

We as believers can dispel nihilism with a few witnesses to the power and love of God.

SPEAK UP if God has changed your life through His ultimate power and grace.

SPEAK UP if you have experienced His mercy.

SPEAK UP if His judgments have converted (transformed, changed) you.

If enough of us stand up and speak up, we will become this great cloud of witnesses who have hoped in God. There will be evidence of a great change in our lives and an increase in our faith.   His judgment has converted us into new creatures in Christ Jesus, and His mercy toward us has been overwhelming. His word should bear fruit in our lives.

The psalmist knew this when he wrote, "Behold the eye of the Lord is on those who fear Him (respect Him), on those who hope in His mercy (unfailing love)" (Psalm 33:18 NIV). One of the prophets named Micah said, "Therefore I will look to the Lord; I will wait for the God of my salvation; my God will hear me" Micah 7:7 (NKJV).

The hope that we have is not misplaced, for the One in whom we hope is completely faithful to His promise. Think about the twelve disciples whom Christ chose in the Bible. They walked with Him and hung on every word He spoke. He talked of a new Kingdom, He spoke with such authority that they believed every word. Can you imagine the despair and hopelessness they experienced when Jesus was killed on the cross?

It is even recorded in the scriptures that they said, "we had hoped that he was the one," the Messiah, the redeemer of the world. For three days, they walked in utter despair.

That is why on the morning of the resurrection they just could not seem to pull themselves out of their hopelessness. They needed a boost. They needed a push.

There were two people walking on the road to Emmaus and they were experiencing hopelessness because their Savior, their hope was gone. Then came Jesus beside them and began to talk with them and He brought hope with Him. Can you imagine the boost when they realized it was Him in whom they had believed? That heavy weight of hopelessness was lifted. It was banished. They could not bring themselves out of it alone. The resurrection made the difference. Now, based on the resurrection, they obtained hope.

God did just what He said He would do. He said, "I come that they might have life and that more abundantly" (John 10:10). Death was the ultimate enemy of hope, but the resurrection was the final blow to break the back of hopelessness.

Hebrew 10:23 admonishes us;

Let us hold fast the confession of our hope without wavering, for he who promised is faithful.

Hope gets you on the starting blocks to total victory. For all of you who might have lost hope, I speak to the spirit of nihilism and command it to release you so that you can grab ahold of hope and hold on tight. Hope will boost you into the realm of faith.

The definition of faith is a belief in, or confident attitude toward God, involving commitment to His will for one's life. Faith can refer to the conviction and ministry of Jesus. True faith is confidence in God and not in oneself. Faith is the essence of the believer's life from beginning to end.[5]

The Land

Now faith is the substances of things hoped
for and the evidence of things not seen.
Hebrews 11:1

WHERE ARE WE NOW in our faith walk?

Beloved, now are we the sons of God and it does
not yet appear what we shall be, but we know that
when he shall appear we shall be like Him for we
shall see Him as He is (I John 3:2).

As believers, we must live in faith, we must speak faith,
but the truth of the matter is we must begin our walk
with faith as the main ingredient to even come to God.
No one can come to God without faith, but we still have
some of the old life in our nature. I call it the "land of
our nativity."

The land of our nativity is full of pride, striving, stress, worry, and getting ahead of others at their expense. All of these are the things that come out of the land of unbelief. We learned that language when we first learned to talk. As children, we are taught to speak the language of our parents and family. They speak of fear, we repeat fear. They speak doubt and worry; we speak of doubt and worry. This is the language of our childhood. This is the language of our nativity. We were "born in sin and shapened in iniquity." The only way we could possibly move out of that land was to be born again.

> Jesus answered and said to him, "Most assuredly, I say to you, unless one is born again, he cannot see the kingdom of God" (John 3:3 NIV).

Once we have the Lord in our lives we gain the ability to see the Kingdom of God. One thing that we must consider is that many of the believers have not fully transitioned over into the land of faith. The land we were naturally born in is full of negativity, unbelief, pride and the works of the flesh. However, we have been given easy access into the land of our new birth.

Ephesians 2:8 states:

> For by grace are ye saved through faith; and that not of yourselves; it is the gift of God.

The land of our new birth is a place of faith. It would be fantastic if, when we were born again, we automatically moved into the land of faith and stayed there. But, unfortunately many do not remain in the land of faith. Instead we revert back to the land of our nativity. Throughout our Christian walk, we tend to move from one dwelling place to another. This happens as significant events occur in our lives.

We move fully into the land of faith when sickness, fear of death, or trouble presents itself. Difficult situations oftentimes, bring us to our knees and we realize that we have no choice but to rely on God. Unfortunately, we frequently jump back and forth between the land of faith and unbelief. We always have a choice. Situations that come into our lives cause us to have to decide where we will go, either to the side of faith or doubt. We all tend to choose faith under stress, but then we go back to our old landmarks when the stress level in our lives diminish.

My husband liked to watch Science Fiction shows on television. I'm not really interested but from time to time I watched with him. One particular evening as I passed through the family room, my husband was watching a show called *Stargate*. I heard the Spirit say, "You need to see this" so I stopped to view the program. Because I began watching in the middle of the story, I really did not understand what was going on.

As I watched, I noticed that there was a huge portal that looked like a circle of blue pulsating plasma. This caught my eye and I began to watch with greater interest. The spaceship had malfunctioned causing the ship to lose power and as a result, the ship's crew was getting sick. A portion of the crew went through this portal and, by passing through it they ended up in a different location. They were searching for something in the ground.

When they found what they were looking for they began to dig the substance up and put it into a large canvas bag. While they were doing this the captain noted that they only had a short window of time in which to gather this material. He began counting down and told the team to pass through the portal before it closed. If it closed while they were on the other side they would not be able to return to the ship. There was one man who found the material they were looking for and was taking a long time dragging it across the desert back to the ship. I'm sure for dramatic emphasis the substance appeared to be very heavy. He couldn't lift it to make it back to the ship. He was determined to get this heavy bag to the ship to save the lives of the crew. All the team members had passed through the portal and time was running out! The captain told the crew that he would not leave the one man behind. The man finally arrived and they both jumped through the circle just as the portal closed. Whew, what an intense scene!

After watching that program, the Lord began to speak to me. He said this is how my children are with faith. When facing a difficult situation, they can move into the realm of faith and actually get results for that time. But, on a regular basis, they slip back to worry and fret, then back to faith, and so on. It is like a roller coaster; up in faith, down in unbelief.

HOW DO WE REMAIN IN THE LAND?

So, how do we remain in this wonderful land called

"Faith?" You are being introduced to the possibilities of this place that God wants us to dwell in and that is an important first step. This kingdom principle of living by faith is shown in the word of God.

The just shall live by faith (Romans 1:17).

To assist you in remaining in the land of faith, I offer some suggestions taken from the book of Jeremiah chapter 29 verse 5; the prophet Jeremiah gives instructions on how to dwell in the new land.

- Build houses
- Settle down
- Plant gardens
- Increase in number

BUILD HOUSES

To build a house in the land of faith implies that you have decided to take up permanent residence there. Building a house means you are expending time, energy and money to make a place of habitation. There is a big difference between building your own house and renting a house from someone else. Renting tends to denote a temporary dwelling. Renters typically are in a place just until they can do better. Renters have certain rights, but they are limited. A homeowner can do anything they please to their home because they own it. They can paint the house any color if permitted by the homeowners association. The owner can customize the mailbox and put their flair on it to tell everyone that you are here for the long haul. The United States government realizes that you are a resident of this land. They deliver all mail to your address.

So, when you get in The Land of Faith, build a house and customize your mailbox out front. Every time you look at your mailbox and your home you know in your heart there is no going back. When you build your house, you have made up your mind to live in The Land of Faith.

SETTLE DOWN

The next step is to settle down. I want to remind you that the land of faith is not heaven. That means that there will be things happening around you, and near you, that might cause you to wonder if you are in the right place. That is why we are in The Land of Faith.

Psalms 91:10 tells us:

because you have made the Lord, who is my refuge, Even the Most High, your dwelling place, no evil shall befall you, nor shall any plague come near your dwelling.

That is a benefit of living in The Land of Faith. There will be things that will tempt you to worry or fret but because of your permanent residence you will not fear. The enemy will always be in there trying to provoke you to doubt or to agitate you to the point of distraction but just keep reminding yourself where you live. You are not here for a visit. Visitors do not have mailboxes and an address at the residence they are visiting. Your address is where you live.

You will know when you are abiding in the land when your language changes. You will begin to speak what the Lord says. "Whose report will you believe?" "We shall believe the report of the Lord" (Isaiah 53:1). His report says I am healed, free, redeemed, protected, saved, cleansed and whole. I could go on and on!

PLANT GARDENS

Next, he said to plant gardens. Planting a garden is another indication that you are here for the long haul. Planting a garden tells everyone including yourself that you plan to remain for a harvest. Planting a garden requires time to prepare the soil to, select seed, plant the seeds, and to oversee the early stages of gardening. This includes watering, proper sunlight, weeding, protecting and then finally harvesting the crops. You will be very busy tending your garden. The fruit of the garden is not just for you and your family. It is a harvest to share with others. Your goal and plan should be to encourage others to move into the land of faith and fully populate it.

Remember the spies that were sent to the land of promise? They were told to take some of the produce back to the children of Israel so they could see that God fulfilled his promise to them. They took back fruit so big that it took two people to carry it. Why did they do that? They were showing signs of fulfillment to encourage the people. Even though giants were in the land, the Lord wanted them to be encouraged that they were well able to secure the land for themselves. This land of faith will produce a great harvest. Because it is not heaven, you will encounter giants and adversity, but at the end of the day, you will be victorious.

The Kingdom of God is voice activated. The prophet Elijah spoke a command that there would be no rain until he said so.

> And Elijah the Tishbite, of the inhabitants of Gilead, said to Ahab, "As the Lord God of Israel lives, before whom I stand, there shall not be dew nor rain these years, except at my word" (I Kings 17:1).

In The Land of Faith, you must say what God says. To say what God says, you must know what God says. That will require a constant diet of the Word of God. That will produce a spiritual vocabulary.

When a nation has been defeated and taken into captivity in a strange land, its conqueror demands they embrace its culture. They want to erase any and all memories of their homeland. They begin with three areas.

- Their look
- Their customs
- Their language

The defeated people are made to comply and assimilate into the culture of the victors by wearing their clothing and styles. The philosophy of the changing of the clothing is to make them fit in. They will walk through the streets of the foreign country and will not be easily identified. They want them to carry the look of the new land. The wearing of the clothing is to say that they are going to live here, not just visit. They are making the unspoken statement, "we are here permanently."

They are then taught to adopt the customs of the new land. They must resist the temptation to retain the customs of their home land. They are now in a new country and they must learn and rehearse the customs. The goal is for them to totally forget the customs of their native land. Some slaves have been so resistant to changing their customs that they practice their homeland customs behind closed doors. They don't want their children to grow up without knowledge of the motherland.

Lastly, is the language. The language must be changed to communicate with the foreign people. This will require more time. Language is the major tool for progress and achievement in the new land. Many slaves learned the new foreign language to use in public, but in the privacy of their homes they continue to speak the language of their homeland.

New birth means we have been moved from the old nature and transcended to new. We are now people of Faith. When we are born again believers we transcend into a new life. The Bible says in II Corthians 5:17 "if any man be in Christ, he is a new creature, old things have passed away, behold all things have become new."

What will happen when we are fully assimilated into The Land of Faith?

FULL ASSIMILATION

First, our thought life will change; Philippians 2:5 states, "Let this mind be in you which was also in Christ Jesus."

Second, your behavior will change; "In all things showing yourself to be a pattern of good works; in doctrine showing integrity, reverence, incorruptibility, sound speech that cannot be condemned, that one who is an opponent may be ashamed, having nothing evil to say of you." Titus 2:7

Third, your language will change; Psalms 19:14, "Let the words of my mouth and the meditation of my heart be acceptable in your sight. O Lord, my strength and my Redeemer."

Speaking what God says, denotes the final change of full assimilation into The Land of Faith. When you start living in The Land of Faith you are going to see things around you change. You are going to start using the authority given to all the residents in the land over small things. Remember, we go from faith to faith. This will increase your confidence in the authority of God's word. Then you will begin to step out into bigger and deeper things.

> I Corinthians 13:11, "When I was a child, I spake as a child, I understood as a child, I thought as a child; but when I became a man I put away childish things."

Oftentimes, you will hear children ask questions such

as: "Daddy I want a cookie, candy, gum, or a story", those are childish things. I Corinthians admonishes us to put childish things away.

As I grow, I speak of deeper things, like:

I command this sickness to leave my body in Jesus name.
I open the door for a job with benefits.
I want to see souls saved.
I want my family redeemed.
I want the healing You promised in Your word.

As you begin to speak healing, deliverance, and banish fears, God will bring the angels to your assistance.

BUILD FAITH

Yes, but how? Obedience to the word and the spirit. Lord give me an ear to hear what the spirit says. Again, you have to know the Word of God, be obedient to what it says in order to have the victory and live in the land of faith. The following scriptures can strengthen you to move into your new home.

Faith comes by hearing and hearing by the word of God (Romans 10:17).

Then He touched their eyes, saying, "According to your faith be it done to you" (Matthew 9:29 ESV).

And he said, "Listen, all you of Judah and you inhabitants of Jerusalem, and you, King

Jehoshaphat! Thus says the LORD to you: 'Do not be afraid nor dismayed because of this great multitude, for the battle is not yours, but God's. Tomorrow go down against them. They will surely come up by the Ascent of Ziz, and you will find them at the end of the brook before the Wilderness of Jeruel. You will not need to fight in this battle. Position yourselves, stand still and see the salvation of the LORD, who is with you, O Judah and Jerusalem!" Do not fear or be dismayed; tomorrow go out against them, for the LORD is with you." And Jehoshaphat bowed his head with his face to the ground, and all Judah and the inhabitants of Jerusalem bowed before the LORD, worshiping the LORD. Then the Levites of the children of the Kohathites and of the children of the Korahites stood up to praise the LORD God of Israel with voices loud and high (II Chronicles 20:15-19).

Rest in the LORD,
and wait patiently for Him;
Do not fret because of him who prospers in his way,
Because of the man who brings wicked schemes to pass. Cease from anger and forsake wrath;
Do not fret—it only causes harm (Psalms 37:7-8).

The heart of the wise teaches his mouth and adds learning to his lips (Proverbs 16:23).

Then Peter said, "Silver and gold I do not have,

but what I do have I give you: In the name of Jesus Christ of Nazareth, rise up and walk" (Acts 3:6 ESV).

LEARNING IN THE LAND

As a retired school teacher, I recall teaching children to improve their reading skills. For many years I taught third grade so most of the children who were in my class already knew how to read at a second-grade level. Coming into third grade, they were going to learn new skills that would take them further in their school career. During our literacy time, I would meet with small groups of children while the rest of the class read independently. I would have them read aloud. Sometimes if they missed a word, I would simply wait for them to realize that they had made a mistake and I taught them how to self-correct. They might have noticed that the sentence they just read did not make sense, or a word they said did not fit in the context of the sentence. They would stop and go back and self-correct. That means they realized their mistake and fixed it by themselves. That is a good sign of a maturing learner.

SAY WHAT GOD SAYS

While you are learning to live in The Land of Faith you might realize that you have stepped back into the land of your nativity. When you realize that you are speaking the language of the motherland, stop immediately, and begin to speak what God says. That is how you self-correct. One of the explicit teachings of the Bible is the importance of the words we speak. Get the word of God in your heart so you can say what He says.

Yadah, is the Hebrew word for confess. It means to open or extend the hands. The idea is to reach out to take hold of something. Just as a closed hand or fist may represent struggle or rebellion, the open hand indicates peace, submitted service or surrender. Confession of God's word is to take a stand on what God says. Speak what is believed with worship and praise.

> So, Jesus answered and said to them, "Have faith in God. For assuredly, I say to you, whoever says to this mountain, 'Be removed and be cast into the sea,' and does not doubt in his heart, but believes that those things he says will be done, he will have whatever he says. Therefore I say to you, whatever things you ask when you pray, believe that you receive them, and you will have them" (Mark 11:22-24).

The Land of Faith is:

STRESS FREE
WORRY FREE
FEAR FREE
ANGER FREE
DOUBT FREE
PRIDE FREE
ENVY FREE
GUILT FREE

It is filled with confidence;

>…my God shall supply all our needs according to
>His riches in glory (Philippians 4:19).

>They shall be My people, and I will be their God;
>then I will give them one heart and one way, that
>they may fear Me forever, for the good of them
>and their children after them. And I will make an
>everlasting covenant with them, that I will not turn
>away from doing them good; but I will put My fear
>in their hearts so that they will not depart from Me
>(Jeremiah 32:38-40).

The Land of Faith is filled with peace;

>Great peace have they which love thy law,
>and nothing shall offend them (Psalms 119:165).

It is filled with love;

>Thou shall love the Lord thy God with all thine
>heart, with all thy soul and with all thy strength
>(Luke 10:27).

**It is filled with trust, total and complete reliance
on God;**

>Trust in the Lord with all thine heart
>and lean not unto thine own understanding,
>in all thy ways acknowledge Him
>and He shall direct your path (Proverbs 3:5-6).

Take a leap into The Land of Faith. Remember the land of faith is not heaven, so there will be trials and trouble but the one thing you have going for you, in the Land of Faith, is that the Lord God of glory is with you and will not forsake you. Jesus told his disciples... "in this world you will have trouble, but take heart I have overcome the world" (John 16:33). And with every trial the Lord will have already made a way of escape and we know that.

Run hard and fast in the faith. Seize the eternal life, the life you were called to, the life you so fervently embraced in the presence of so many witnesses. I Tim. 6:12 MSG

Adventures In the Land of Faith

I have glorified You [down here] on the earth by completing the work that You gave me to do.
John 17:4 (AMP)

WELL, NOW THAT WE HAVE MADE our trek into the lan how are you feeling? It is exciting and a little scar at the same time. Why is that? Because you have entere a place of the unknown. You might want to rehearse som testimonies of what has happened since we have leape into The Land of Faith.

So when Jesus had received the sour wine, He said, " is finished!" And bowing His head He gave up His spir (John 19:30).

The phrase "it is finished" means a work was complete on the cross fulfilling the requirements of God for the sou of humanity. "It is finished, or it is paid." It frequent signifies, not merely to terminate a thing, but to carry o a thing to completion.

Jesus saith unto them, "My meat is to do the will of him that sent me, and to finish his work" (John 4:34).

I have glorified thee on the earth; I have finished the work which thou gavest me to do (John 17:4).

WHAT WAS JESUS SENT TO DO?

JESUS, meaning *God is Savior* was sent to be the Savior of the world to everyone that would believe.

CHRIST, meaning *the anointed one*, shows us that He was given a special assignment to direct the lives of his followers.

SON OF MAN identifies him as Messiah, the promised redeemer.

SON OF GOD, speaks to his supernatural birth. This is a miraculous birth and fulfillment of the holy scripture.

LORD means He has authority and ownership.

He was sent to bring mankind into the right relationship with God and to allow mankind to fulfill our purpose, from before the foundation of the world. The hindrance was sin, which started with the first man Adam. God wanted to bring man back to the place of deep relationship with Him just like Adam had enjoyed in the garden. The Bible says:

Everything man needed to be a son of God was provided through Jesus Christ. Christ gave himself for the church, that he might sanctify and cleanse it with the washing of water by the word (Ephesians 5:26).

When this scripture says "everything" it means everything:

- Salvation
- Healing
- Deliverance
- Power
- Authority
- Glory
- Deep relationship
- Joy

Once you have arrived in The Land of Faith you must put down roots. You now have an address and a mailbox. There are certain declarations that must be made daily. When we read the word, there are things in the word of God that we must claim even though it sounds way out there.

The angel of the Lord came to Mary as a young girl who was only about 14 years old. The message that was given to her was that of the promised Messiah. The fact that she was not married and was a virgin made the word even more out of the realm of rational thinking. The words that come out of our mouths are very important. They can bring life and strength or death and destruction. Remember the Kingdom of God is voice activated.

Then Mary said, "Behold the maidservant of the Lord! Let it be to me according to your word." And the angel departed from her (Luke 1:38).

"Be it," means to be made, or finished. Mary called herself, "handmaid of the Lord." "I am under your authority and will do as you say." She makes a declaration- "be it unto me." Under one condition- "at thy word."

Stablish thy word unto thy servant, who is devoted to thy fear (Psalm 119:38).

So, shall My word be that goes forth from My mouth; It shall not return to Me void, But it shall accomplish what I please, And it shall prosper in the thing for which I sent it (Isaiah 55:11 NKJV).

When God says something, He will make it good. Take steps into The Land of Faith.

- Faith is substance
- Faith will hold you up
- Faith will not fail
- Have faith in God
- With God, nothing shall be impossible.

As you walk in The Land of Faith you will begin to hear God more clearly, and as you hear Him, His voice will get stronger. He will begin to lead you into deep water. Also, begin to write in a journal about the adventures you are having in The Land of Faith.

I started a business that helped people with invention ideas. The name of the business was Jael. I had received some outstanding ideas and I was anxious to locate companies that would buy the ideas and develop them into products that would be available to the public. One of my clients had an invention that I thought a major pharmaceutical company would have interest in. I met a lady who worked for this company and she told me that I could not get into the building without being invited by one of the employees. It is a very secure company. So, I "wrote off" that company from being one that I could get in to share our product.

One day I was praying, and I heard the Spirit of the Lord tell me to get ready and go to this particular company. He gave me very specific instructions as I prepared to go to the company that I had formerly been unable to enter. Just before I walked out of the door, I heard the Lord say, look up the executives that work there. I carefully scrolled down the personnel directory and found the names of a couple of people. I wrote their names on a notepad and stuck it in my pocket.

I drove to the company and pulled up to the parking garage. I was met by a young security guard who proceeded to inform me that I could not enter the garage without an appointment. I was sad because I believed that God had sent me to this place. While we stared at one another she said, "do you at least have the name of someone that works here?" At that question, I pulled the notepad out of my pocket and read the names I had written down. When I read those names the gate immediately opened, and I drove into the restricted garage. When I parked, the same security guard said, "you are a classy lady but if you don't have an appointment you won't get past the next guard." I politely thanked her and walked to the door.

Just before I arrived at the door, the security guard that was watching the door received a phone called and he walked away from the door, providing me with access to the building without being challenged. I entered the building that I was not supposed to get in and I walked up to the receptionist at her desk. She asked me the same question as the first security guard. To which I rattled of the names I had on my note pad. She then admitted me to the lobby house phones. I looked up the phone numbers of the employees that I had on my pad. I then placed a call to their secretaries. I asked for an appointment and they each were out of the office, but they took my name and number and said that I could call back to set an appointment at a later time.

After finishing that task, I needed to use the restroom. So, I asked the receptionist if she would please direct me to the nearest one. She said, "yes, but you will have to check your purse and go through the metal detector." I went through the metal detector and was then given a pass that gave me access to the entire building. With my pass, I stepped into massive areas that were restricted. I went into the restroom, which was gorgeous by the way, and was located right by the elevators. None of the guards were watching me and I could have easily gotten on the elevator without being accosted. When I came out of the restroom, I gave the pass back and signed out of the building. I got into my car and drove out of the place I was told I could not gain entrance to.

The Lord began to deal with me concerning this entire event and showed me that faith can open the doors that everyone says are closed. Faith says, "nevertheless at thy WORD." The same way those doors were opened, God will open the doors that need to be opened for you. I was walking in The Land of Faith even before I totally understood the concept.

Abraham also had adventures in The Land of Faith. God spoke a word to him about having a son in his old age. Abraham laughed. God spoke the same words to his wife Sarah and she laughed too. "How could this be? How could God perform such a miracle with us?" they thought. But with God all things are possible. When you are in The Land of Faith you will do what Abraham did. It is recorded in the book of Romans 4:20, "He staggered not at the promise of God through unbelief; but was strong in faith, giving glory to God."

What is God saying to you? You must step out in faith and obey His voice. Peter, one of the disciples in the Bible who would later help start the early church understood the principle of faith. When Jesus asked him to come, he got out of his boat. He was not standing on water, he was standing on faith in the word, "come". He was walking on that "come," and the only reason he began to sink was because the word was no longer his primary focus.

FAITH IS SUBSTANCE

Don't look at the odds that are stacked against you. Listen to what God told you. Get out the prophetic word that you know was just for you. Get it out and begin to read it over and over. Get in the Word and begin to stand on what it says. You will see that it will hold you up and you can go far on that Word.

REMEMBER THE POWER OF HIS WORD

HIS WORD HEALS

The psalmist said, "He sent His word and healed them, And delivered them from their destructions" (Psalms 107:20). This means, taking the Word of God into your heart can actually heal you. Get the Word in you. You can read it, listen to it on a podcast or app, listen to it being preached, or watch it on television, however you find is the best way to get the Word. By all means necessary get the Word. It brings healing not only for your soul but for your body as well.

HIS WORD CLEANSES

that He might sanctify and cleanse her with the washing of water by the word (Eph. 5:26 NKJV).

This cleansing is the cleansing of the soul. Our souls need daily cleansing to stay on top of the spiritual pollution that can be deposited into our souls. Things we see and hear can begin to pollute our souls, but the Word of God brings a washing that takes these pollutants out of our souls. Thanks be to God, who has given us everything that pertains to life and Godliness.

You are already clean because of the word which I have spoken to you (John 15:3).

HIS WORD LAUNCHES

When He had stopped speaking, He said to Simon, "Launch out into the deep and let down your nets for a catch" (Luke 5:4).

His Word protects

Every word of God is pure;
He is a shield to those who put their trust in Him
(Proverbs 30:5).

His Word covers

And I have put My words in your mouth; I have
covered you with the shadow of My hand, That I
may plant the heavens, Lay the foundations of the
earth, And say to Zion, "You are My people"(Isaiah
51:16).

His Word rescues

Because he has set his love upon Me,
therefore I will deliver him;
I will set him on high, because he has known My
name. He shall call upon Me, and I will answer
him;
I will be with him in trouble;
I will deliver him and honor him (Psalms 91:14-15).

His Word restores

The law of the LORD is perfect,
converting the soul;
The testimony of the LORD is sure,
making wise the simple; (Psalms 19:7)

His Word creates

Then God said, "Let there be light"; and there was
light (Genesis 1:3).

HIS WORD CONVICTS

John 16:8 "And when He has come, He will convict the world of sin, and of righteousness, and of judgment:"

HIS WORD ACCOMPLISHES

Psalms 147:15 "He sends out His command to the earth; His word runs very swiftly."

HIS WORD PROSPERS

Isaiah 55:11 "So shall My word be that goes forth from My mouth; It shall not return to Me void, But it shall accomplish what I please, And it shall prosper in the thing for which I sent it."

HIS WORD GUIDES

Psalms 119:105 "Your word is a lamp to my feet and a light to my path.

Some years ago, Walter Hawkins wrote a song entitled "Changed." His wife, Tremaine Hawkins, sang it and many people were blessed by this tremendous song.

Changed

A change, a change has come over me,
He changed my life and now I'm free
He washed away all my sins and he made me whole
He washed me, white as snow.
He changed my life complete
and now I sit, I sit at His feet,
To do what must be done
I'll work and work until he comes.
A wonderful change has come over me.
A wonderful change has come over me.
Lord He changed, my life complete
And now I sit at my Savior's feet
He changed my walk
He changed my talk
He even changed my thoughts
I'm not what I want to be
I'm not what I use to be
I'm not the same
A wonderful change has come over me.

Topography is the study and mapping of the features on the surface of the land, including natural features such as mountains and rivers, and constructed features such as highways and railroads. The scenery, landscape and countryside.[6]

Topography of the Land of Faith

There is a river whose stream make glad the city of
God. The holy dwelling places of the Most High.
Psa. 46:4

I HAVE TAUGHT ABOUT THE TOPOGRAPHY of The Land c
Faith for a long time. We might not have thought of
in this way but in the church, we have even written song
about the landscape of the Christian experience:

> **The Cleansing stream**, *I see, I see, I plunged and
> Oh it cleanseth me. O praise the Lord it cleanseth me. By
> Phoebe Palmer*

> **There is a river** *that flows from God above. There is
> a fountain that is filled with His great love. Come to these
> waters, there is a vast supply. There is a river that never
> shall run dry. By Gaither Vocal Band*

> **There is a fountain** *filled with blood, drawn from
> Emmanuel's veins. And sinners plunge beneath the flood*

lose all their guilty stains, lose all their guilty stains. And sinners plunge beneath the flood lose all their guilty stains. Written by William Cowper

For Every Mountain *you've brought me over, for every trial you've seen me through. For every blessing, Hallelujah for this I give you praise. By Kurt Carr*

I'm pressing on the Upward Way- *Lord lift me up and let me stand, by faith on Canaan's tableland. A higher plane than I have found, Lord plant my feet on higher ground. By Johnson Oatman, Jr. & Charles Hutchinson Gabriel*

Rivers are defined as large streams of water emptying into an ocean, lakes or other bodies of water are usually fed along its course by smaller streams.[7] Rivers served as ideal places for cities and settlements, as well as religious events, such as baptisms.

In The Land of Faith rivers are very important as well. There you can be refreshed. You can take long rests, drink the water, and be sustained for your journey. The river has an abundant supply of everything you need to eat and to drink. The Bible describes in Matthew 3:6:

Then Jerusalem, all Judea, and all the region around the Jordan went out to him and were baptized by him in the Jordan, confessing their sins. Another example would be the healing of Naaman by dipping into the river at the instructions of the man of God. And his servants came near and spoke to him, and said, "My father, if the prophet had told you to do something great, would you not have done it? How much more then, when he says to you, 'Wash, and be clean'?" So he went down and dipped seven times in the Jordan, according to the saying of the man of God; and his flesh was restored like the flesh of a little child, and he was clean (II Kings 5:13-14 NKJV).

In the beginning of the record of mankind, it is recorded that there were five rivers that came out of the garden of Eden. These rivers represented God's abundant provision for the fertility of the garden.

Now a river went out of Eden to water the garden, and from there it parted and became four riverheads. The name of the first is Pishon; it is the one which skirts the whole land of Havilah, where there is gold. And the gold of that land is good. Bdellium and the onyx stone are there. The name of the second river is Gihon; it is the one which goes around the whole land of Cush. The name of the third river is Hiddekel; it is the one which goes toward the east of Assyria. The fourth river is the Euphrates (Genesis 2:10-14).

I am going to make a spiritual application of the natural topography found in the Word of God as a source of divine blessings.

There is a river whose
    streams shall make glad
    the city of God,

The holy place of the tabernacle
of the Most High (Psalms 46:4).

Again he measured one thousand, and it was a river
that I could not cross; for the water was too deep,
water in which one must swim, a river that could
not be crossed. He said to me, "Son of man, have
you seen this?" Then he brought me and returned
me to the bank of the river. When I returned, there,
along the bank of the river, were very many trees on
one side and the other. Then he said to me: "This
water flows toward the eastern region, goes down
into the valley, and enters the sea. When it reaches
the sea, its waters are healed. And it shall be that
every living thing that moves, wherever the rivers
go, will live. There will be a very great multitude
of fish, because these waters go there; for they will
be healed, and everything will live wherever the
river goes. It shall be that fishermen will stand by
it from En Gedi to En Eglaim; they will be places
for spreading their nets. Their fish will be of the
same kinds as the fish of the Great Sea, exceedingly
many. But its swamps and marshes will not be
healed; they will be given over to salt. Along the
bank of the river, on this side and that, will grow
all kinds of trees used for food; their leaves will not
wither, and their fruit will not fail. They will bear
fruit every month, because their water flows from
the sanctuary. Their fruit will be for food, and their
leaves for medicine (Ezekiel 47:5-12).

Regarding the heavenly Jerusalem, Revelation 22:1-2 :

> And he showed me a pure river of water of life, clear as crystal, proceeding from the throne of God and of the Lamb. In the middle of its street, and on either side of the river, was the tree of life, which bore twelve fruits, each tree yielding its fruit every month...

The word "river" is also used to symbolize God's delights. In the Old Testament living water or flowing rivers stand for God's faithfulness and lasting provision for his people.[8] In Psalms 36:8 it says, "They are abundantly satisfied with the fullness of Your house, And You give them drink from the river of Your pleasures." Other symbols of rivers in the scriptures are:

- **Peace-**   Oh, that you had heeded My commandments! Then your peace would have been like a river, And your righteousness like the waves of the sea (Isaiah 48:18).

- **Life-** He who believes in Me, as the Scripture has said, out of his heart will flow rivers of living water (John 7:38).

- **Tears-** My eyes overflow with rivers of water For the destruction of the daughter of my people (Lamentations 3:48).

The word also illustrates God's providential control over nature in Psalms 107:33 " He turns rivers into a wilderness and the watersprings into dry ground;"

In the Bible rivers are symbolic of many things;

- **Location**- the rivers went out from the garden of Eden boundaries- the waters went from river to river creating boundaries (Genesis 2:10-14).

- **Safety**- the water was a place where the Lord told them they could pass over (Joshua 1-24).

- **Places of Contemplation**- Pharaoh was standing by a river in a dream when God gave him a dream concerning the nation of Egypt (Genesis 41:17).

- **Cleansing**- Naaman was the captain of the host of Syria and the prophet told him to dip in the Jordan river seven times and he would be clean. John the Baptist was baptizing people in the Jordan river while they confessed their sins (II Kings 5).

- **Death**- In the book of Exodus many children of Israel were cast into the river because Pharaoh was looking to kill Moses who was prophesied to be the deliverer of the nation (Exodus 1:22).

- **Salvation**- The same river that killed many children was the same river that saved Moses because God had planned for this child to be the deliverer of Israel (Exodus 2:1-10).

- **Hope and Uncertainty**- Ezra, who was a priest and scribe for God in Israel, shared the facts that there were kings that ruled, and they did not want these kings to gain a foothold ever again. So, the order went out to cease from rebuilding the city (Ezra 4:1-23).

- **Abundance-** In the book of Job the water speaks of washing your steps with butter pouring out rivers of oil (Job 29:6).

- **Continual Blessings-** You shall be planted by the rivers of water which will cause you to bring forth fruit in your season and whatsoever you do will prosper. In John he says out of your belly shall flow rivers of living water (John 7:38).

- **Everlasting Joy and Glory-** And he showed me a pure river of water of life clear as crystal, proceeding out of the throne of God and of the Lamb this speaks of the eternal river that God provides from the beginning unto the end of time (Revelation 22:1).

TYPOGRAPHY IN THE LAND

Within the topography or scenery, landscape or countryside of The Land of Faith, you will encounter mountains, valleys, hills, quicksand, cliffs, pasture land, meadows, dry parched land, sink holes, waterfalls, pools, streams, oceans and rivers.

RIVERS

You see, every child of God who enters The Land of Faith will experience many, if not all, of the topographies of this place. You might think that The Land of Faith has no negative encounters or issues that require trust in God or the need to cry out to Him. On the contrary, you are going to come to rivers which either may separate you from something that could bring you pain or grief, or that will be the vehicle that will carry you over to the other side. Make no mistake about this land, you will encounter hills and mountains; not to discourage you but to strengthen you and develop a deeper knowledge of God. You will come to understand that if He does not give you the strength and the command to traverse the mountain then He will prompt you to say to this mountain, "...be thou removed and be cast into the sea, and it will have to obey you" (Mark 11:23). The Bible is replete with bodies of water representing spiritual stages and so it is in The Land of Faith.

ANKLE DEEP

In Ezekiel, he speaks of the depth of the river. This river represents the healing and life-giving power of the Holy Spirit. No matter how deep you want to go into the things of God, the opportunity is there to go even deeper. It's tragic that too many Christians linger in the shallows when they could be enjoying the depths. Ankle deep experiences are for the newbies in the land. These are the people who want to walk in The Land of Faith but have just begun. It does not matter how old you are. When you realize that there is another place in God that is accessible to you, you launch out.

At first the water is only ankle deep. This gives you a little time to enjoy your new-found land. This is where you sense God's presence frequently and things are going well. Prayers are answered immediately. You are singing the songs of Zion every day. Ankle deep is great because it develops the sweet relationship between you and the Master.

Do you remember when you first wanted to swim? You kind of laid in the water with your head above the surface and you walked on your hands kicking the water with your feet. That was a fun way to move through the water, but you were not really swimming. You didn't let any water get in your face, which might cause some major fear, and you might have even gotten out of the water for a while.

In the spirit realm where The Land of Faith exists, you know beyond the shadow of a doubt you are not going to drown. No matter what you go through, He will bring you out with victory. How do I know that? Because God promised it in His word and "God is not a man that he should lie." The operative word here is ***through***. This is where you practice listening and obeying His voice. You go from glory to glory, from faith to faith. Even though you can stand up and walk, you chose to lay in the water and allow the Lord to guide you through. This is taking the fear of the water away. These exercises are building you for the next level. Your song is, "Where he leads, me I will follow." There might be some disappointments and some trials, but He will always bring you through. In Ezekiel he said, "HE brought me through" which denotes a continual progression (emphasis by me). You cannot stay where everything is always good, there must be some adversity in order to yield a robust character and faith. Just remember, He brought me through!

KNEE DEEP

Let's go a little further where the water came to his knees. This is a closer walk and it might even create a little difficulty to walk but you can still move. Knee experiences are truly walking in the Spirit. There are trials and problems, but you can always find the way through them. God is leading you through them all. These are times when you will have to learn the sound of His voice and trust what He is saying.

WASTE DEEP

Now when the water is at the waist, the experiences are a little more intense. This is a deeper relationship with the Lord. It is getting a little more difficult to move quickly. You must walk slower and more deliberately. It is easier to fall in waist high water. You can lose control much more easily. In waist deep water you can swim, but you also can stand if things get a little wearisome. You can always rely on your own feet or we might say your own ability. Even though you are in the water and swimming is the preferred mode of transportation, you can still walk if you like.

WATERS TO SWIM IN

Then there were the "waters to swim in." These waters do not provide any means of standing on our own. This level requires total dependency on the Master. However, you have been well acquainted with Him because of the previous levels of anointing and glory that you have enjoyed. He teaches you all sorts of swimming techniques to navigate the waters. Treading water, backstroke, sidestroke, breaststroke and floating, all are needed in the "waters to swim in."

Those who do business in great waters
will see the works of the Lord,
and his wonders in the deep
(Psalms 107:23).

   Fear plays no part in the residents of The Land of Faith. Do not fear the deep. You will see things that are reserved for the special ones who will launch out. If you have been longing to see the works of the Lord, then you must go into the deep water. You want to see miracles or even participate in them? They are found in deep water.

CANYONS

   Then you come to those canyons. You know the ones that are sometimes referred to as mountain passes. They are so narrow that you can barely make it through. The ones where you have to take off every bit of equipment, including your backpack and water bottle in order to get through the opening. The canyon is where you can't see anything but sheer mountain sides with high walls of rock.

   The only thing you can see is what lies straight in front of you. This tight place is only for a little while, so keep walking. The mountain passes can feel lonely and tight, almost claustrophobic at times. Keep walking. You feel kind of vulnerable in the valley because your enemy could be on top of the mountain and ambush you with no way to escape. Don't let your imagination get the best of you. Cast down that imagination and bring into captivity every thought to the obedience of Christ. Okay that's better. Before you start feeling miserable and terrified, look ahead and see there is a broad open place.

STREAMS

There are streams of refreshing water. God calls it "living water." Take a drink and be renewed. Oh look, there is lush green grass so thick and soft you can take your shoes off and let your feet slide over the soft moist grass. Now look, there is a place just right for you to lay down, and beside the grass is a brook of clean, fresh, cold water. Sit here awhile and rest. Listen to the sweet songs of the birds that only sing in the canyon. In the canyon, you thought you would find dread but instead you find peace and tranquility. There are people who have dreaded the valley because they thought there was nothing in the canyon for them. We have songs about the mountain but in the canyon, you receive restoration and strength. The song says *"in the valley he restores my soul."*

In the
valley
He restores
my
Soul

Faith That 5 Moves God

Now faith is the substance of things hoped for, the
evidence of things not seen. For by it the elders
obtained a good testimony. By faith we
understand that the worlds were framed
by the word of God, so that what is seen
was not made out of what was visible.
Hebrews 11:1-3

THERE IS A FAITH that will cause God to lean forward
and move on your behalf. This is the faith that will
produce.

Then Jesus went out from there and departed to the
region of Tyre and Sidon. And behold, a woman
of Canaan came from that region and cried out to
Him, saying, "Have mercy on me, O Lord, Son of
David! My daughter is severely demon-possessed."
But He answered her not a word. And His disciples
came and urged Him, saying, "Send her away, for
she cries out after us." But He answered and said,

"I was not sent except to the lost sheep of the house of Israel." Then she came and worshiped Him, saying, "Lord, help me!" But He answered and said, "It is not good to take the children's bread and throw it to the little dogs." And she said, "Yes, Lord, yet even the little dogs eat the crumbs which fall from their masters' table." Then Jesus answered and said to her, "O woman, great is your faith! Let it be to you as you desire." And her daughter was healed from that very hour" (Matthew 15:21-28).

What kind of woman was this that was crying after Jesus? A Syrophoenician woman, a Greek woman. I think we need to take a good look at this woman. Even though she was a Gentile, she must have heard something about Jesus that moved her to go outside her circle of friends and to enter into a possible breach of the law at that time. In this culture, women were not respected or given many rights during this time. To touch a man that was not either her father, brother or husband was unheard of, but to touch a rabbi, she was putting herself in even more danger. She touched a man that was very different from herself.

First, she cried after the Lord. That means she shouted and hollered after Jesus, but Jesus kept moving and did not stop to give her any attention. Crying did not move Him. She cried and shouted," have mercy or take pity on me." Crying brings release to your soul when you are under pressure. Crying helps you feel better, helps produce a feeling of cleansing within. Crying can be an expression of joy, anger, extreme laughter, or sorrow.

Crying is usually triggered by some event. Crying has its place within human emotion because Psalms 34:6 states, "This poor man cried out, and the LORD heard him, And saved him out of all his troubles." There are times when crying can get results, however, at this time, with this woman, crying did not get Jesus to stop and answer her or meet her needs. His response; "He answered her not a word." In spite of the crying, she did not get any answer from the Lord. Have you ever cried and seemingly not gotten any response from the Lord?

Her Action:

She went to the disciples and cried. Humility is important in the life of a believer. The humble person is not proud or haughty, not arrogant or assertive, reflecting, expressing or offered in a spirit of deference or submission.[9] The Word of God says, "we humble ourselves with fasting and lower ourselves before someone greater" (Isaiah 58:1). To humble yourself brings exaltation. I Peter 5:6 says,"Humble yourselves under the mighty hand of God, that He may exalt you in due time."

When you engage in true worship you will notice that there might be people kneeling because they recognize that they are before someone greater and they humble themselves. It is not just an outward manifestation, but those actions reflect what is happening inwardly.

There are several positions that represent humbling yourself in the Bible:

- Covering your face
- Bowing on your knees

- Bowing your head
- Bowing your upper body so that your forehead touches the floor or the ground
- Walking around in sack cloth and putting ashes on your head

Disciples' Response:

They sent her away because they felt she was bothering them. You know there will be times when others just don't get what you need from the Lord. They might make statements like, "it doesn't take all that", or "they have been to the altar two Sundays in a row." You have to press past thoughts and opinions of others. Notice, this woman keeps coming.

Jesus' Response:

This mighty God man does not say, "come here my daughter," or, "what can I do for you, I see that you are broken and in great distress." No, He says, "I am sent to the house of Israel." What? You mean the one that has my answer for my daughter is telling me that His mission is to another group of people that I am not a part of?

Her Response:

She begins to worship him and says, "Lord help me!" She is getting closer to the response that the Lord is looking for. By saying, "Lord help me," she acknowledges His Lordship, the Holy one, Adonai, Almighty God, Sovereign Lord, Deliverer, Savior, Master. You are the only one that can do anything for me. She's saying, "I know you can help me and I will worship and bow before you because I have a need."

Let's look at a couple of Biblical historical characters in the word of God. Let's look at Job. The Bible refers to Job as a man who fears and honors God. It sounds like he was a man who loved God and obeyed. When reading this book you can see that the blessings of the Lord were released to him and his family. When Job's life was going well we read that he prayed for himself and his family. Then as we continue to read we find that God allowed Satan to attack Job and his family. When the attack on his family was completed where is Job? He is worshipping the Lord. He is not accusing God for all his losses, he is not reminding God of how good he was, he is not comparing himself to others, he says, "the Lord gives and the Lord takes away, blessed be the name of the Lord." What??? You mean to tell me that Job worshipped in the middle of his trauma and trouble? Yes, that is a demonstration of his faith. When you read the end of his story God moved in his life and Job's last days were more blessed than before his trouble started. That is a faith that moves God.

Let's take a look at the Hebrew boys. These are three men whose faith in God was unmatched. The decree went out in Babylon that everyone must bow down and worship a golden image that the king had erected. This was idol worship. If disobeyed it would mean death. The Hebrews boys were only sure of one thing and that is that they were committed to the true and living God and they were not going to worship an image. The outcome of their decision was up to God, they knew he was able to deliver them from the burning fiery furnace but did not know if he would deliver them. The faith that moved God is this story allowed them to go into the furnace but not be burned and they gave all glory to God.

I want to share just one more instance of two people in the Bible who moved God with their faith. Paul and Silas were locked in prison. Not sure of their fate, but at midnight they began to pray and sing praises unto God. They just did what came natural to a spiritual person. In the midst of the worship the Lord released an earthquake that was so specialized that it only shook the prison doors open and loosed the chains that were on the prisoner's arms and legs. Talking about a faith that moves God which can achieve results without begging. All you need to do is worship and agree with God about the situation.

Worship will get God's attention however you need a response.

Jesus' Response:

HE stops and speaks to her. Well, that is a start. At least she got Him to finally stop. But He reminds her of her position and low estate in the Hebrew culture. You are a Gentile, you are a "dog," you are not part of the chosen people. You are not in line for the blessings that are promised to the children Israel.

Her Response:

"Truth Lord!" What? she agreed with him. She does not offer any argument. She did not get insulted nor did she turn around and walk away in a huff. Agreement is very powerful and is a law in the Kingdom of God. The Law of Agreement works.

Matthew 18:19 says,

> Again I say to you that if two of you agree on earth concerning anything that they ask, it will be done for them by My Father in heaven.

Agreement produces faith, which comes by hearing and hearing by the Word of God.

AGREEMENT PRODUCES FAITH

We must agree with His word. When He says, "you shall be the above only and not the beneath," you must agree. When He says, "for the promise is unto you and to your children and to as many as the Lord or God shall call," you must agree. When He says, "by His stripes you are healed" you must agree, when He says "without holiness no man shall see the Lord", you must agree. When he says, "righteousness exalts a nation, but sin is a reproach to any people", you must agree. When He says, "when the enemy comes, in like a flood the spirit of the Lord will lift up a standard against it", you must agree. When He says, "great peace have they which love thy law and nothing shall by any means hurt you", you must agree. When He says, "I can do all things through Christ which strengthens me", agree with Him. When He says, "No weapon formed against you shall prosper"- Agree. When He says, "the just shall live by faith"-with your whole heart, you must agree!

So, after being ignored and insulted, what was the outcome? She received a commendation from the Lord. He tells her," you have great faith." Her faith pushed her into another dimension. She spoke that the word would bring the deliverance needed for healing. That very hour agreement produced faith. So, what moves God? Agreement! Agreement with the word of God.

Faith comes by hearing and hearing by the word of God (Rom. 10:17).

Don't just agree with your mouth, agree with God in your heart. Agreement produces the faith necessary for manifestation.

If God calls you a sinner, **Agree** with Him, and faith will arise to deliver you from your sin and save your soul.

Oh, but what if God says you are in a state of Laodicea? **Agree**.

If God says repent- **Agree**.

If God says, stand still and see the salvation of the Lord- **Agree.**

The Syrophoenician woman's faith pushed her into another dimension. A special place of confidence where she had never been before with circumstances that prompted her to move beyond what was familiar or comfortable. She began to speak prophetically. She said that the Gentiles would be able to come into the house. What, those Gentile dogs? How dare her speak such an unbelievable thought. Then she went even further. She mentioned that the Gentiles would be under the authority of the Lord Jesus Christ. What, these dogs will follow the Lord and He will become their King? She spoke that the Gentiles would be partakers of the Word of God. Oh, my goodness she has gone too far now! You mean to tell me that Gentiles will not only get to read but also believe the Word of God? We thought this precious Word was preserved only for the Jews. The holy Word of God was only for the Jews, right? Then she continued to prophecy and say that the Word would bring deliverance and liberation needed to heal. "Let it be to you as you desire." And her daughter was healed from that very hour.

From the moment your agreement produces faith, that is the very hour when you grab the Word and hold on to it for dear life. Once you test this out, you will see that the agreement with the word releases such power that you will choose to constantly walk in this dimension because your eyes will be open.

The power of sight: The human eye is the lens and film of the most advanced camera in the world. It offers stunning clarity and vivid colors; focusing, adjusting and capturing images literally in the blink of an eye.[10]

We Walk

For we walk by faith, and not by sight. II Cor. 5:7

While we do not look at the things which are
seen, but at the things which are not seen. For
the things which are seen are temporary, but
the things which are not seen are eternal.
II Cor. 4:18

A SIMPLE SMILE FROM A LOVED ONE can warm the heart.
This sentence is translated from mere single characters
into a deeper meaning by the visual information signaling
from behind your eyes to your brain. Movement of the
hand and arm to reach for a cup of coffee is effortless
because information is passed to the brain from the eye.
While walking along a busy street while shopping, our
eyes warn us of oncoming crowds, working in conjunction
with our brain, this allows us to navigate a safe path. The
sight of our favorite food stimulates our appetite and
activates our salivary glands. These are just some of the
millions of ways our mind, emotions and activities are
influenced by our vision.

We have been trained to believe what we see. There is an old saying, "seeing is believing." But today that is one thing we must wipe out of our thinking. There are so many ways for images to be created, through Photoshop, digital imagery, picture enhancements, filters, etc. You really cannot believe what you see! Your image can actually be inserted into a photograph with people that you don't know and show you present at an event, even when you know you were never actually there.

In The Land of Faith, our thought process must be just the opposite. Abraham is the father of faith. We must follow our father Abraham and do it just like he did.

> By faith he forsook Egypt, not fearing the wrath of the king; for he endured as seeing Him who is invisible (Hebrew 11:27).

I am convinced that when we are walking in The Land of Faith there will be forces that will try to pull us away from our solid faith stance.

THINGS THAT OUR EYES SEE

Not all of our possessions are demonic or evil. Some of the things that lure us away are attractive things, necessary things. They are things that will not harm you. However, they are possessions that will distract us from the walk which God has called each of us to.

The faith walk is amazing. Some of the things that our eyes might see that could cause our faith to waver are sickness. If you are declaring that a person is going to be healed by the blood of Jesus Christ and day after day your eyes tamper with your faith because you see that person steadily getting worse. You almost have to close your eyes and stand on the Word of God. Maybe your eyes see an empty refrigerator and cabinets. Your ears hear your children crying due to hunger pains. It takes an extra push in the faith realm to look past their hunger and see Jehovah Jireh, the provider bringing you what you need just in the nick of time. Listen, your eyes will cause you to doubt the voice of God. Many times you hear God clearly but the circumstances surrounding you will say something different and now here you are in the valley of decision.

I heard a story told by a well known minister. He said that one morning he heard the voice of God tell him to go by some groceries. These groceries were not for him and his family. They were for someone else but he did not know who at the time. He and his wife obeyed God and bought the groceries. Then he began to drive around different neighborhoods waiting for God to point out the person who needed the food. He stopped a lady and asked her if she needed any food. She said no, but you must be talking about Mrs. Brown. She pointed him to her apartment. He went to the door and a lady opened up the door and he saw four little children sitting on the sofa. He later found out that these children were given to her as a result of her negligent daughter. He asked her if she needed food and she began to smile and said, "yes". She invited them in and told them the story of how these children became her responsibility. She then began to praise God and tell the children," I told you God would provide food for us." When we walk by faith everything is not perfect, but God works in imperfect situations.

If you look with your natural eye you just might miss the miracle that God wants to present to you. Sometimes holding on to things can cause you to miss the greater blessing that God has planned. Often God will nudge you to let go of something, you do that by faith because you don't see what God is up to. Some of our possessions can be a hindrance to our faith walk. Not all of our possessions are demonic or evil. Some of the things that distract you away from our faith stance are not always bad things or attractive things, but sometimes they are necessary things. They are not things that will not harm you. Think of it this way, have you ever been distracted while driving a car? I'm pretty sure you know the danger in getting distracted. We do not even have to mention driving and texting but what about dropping something on the floor while driving? It is so easy to look away for just a split second and reach for the item. This small distraction could cause an accident. Likewise walking by faith and allowing things to distract you could cost you.

THE WALK OF FAITH

Try this small activity, get a blind fold and put it on and have a friend that you trust give you directions that you will follow merely by listening to the voice of your friend. This is how you are going to have to walk if you are going to walk by faith. Faith is not seeing, faith is listening to the voice of the Lord and doing what he says. Walking by faith and not by sight.

This blind fold will help you block out the things that hinder you from hearing God's voice. Abraham heard the voice of God and then he moved.

While we do not look at the things which are seen, but at the things which are not seen. For the things which are seen are temporary, but the things which are not seen are eternal (II Corinthians 4:18).

One of the best ways to listen is to close your eyes. The best way to block out distractions is to focus on the voice. We tweet, we text, we email. Everybody's chatting, but is anybody listening?

In the land of our nativity we are taught that if we stop and listen to a person is not an efficient use of our time. We rarely look at a person while they speak to get the full essence of their language. It is quickly causing us to lose the ability to talk and listen from our hearts. Unfortunately, that is exactly what could happen when you are conversing with the Lord. We are moving at such a pace that we are not stopping to listen to Him. If we can't hear Him then we are forced to use another sense, that of sight. We move on what we see instead of what we hear. If we happen to step back into the land of our nativity and realize where we are, we need to stop and self-correct. Get back into The Land of Faith and wait for the voice of the Lord. I know waiting is very hard to do. But remember that you are not just sitting and doing nothing while you are waiting. You wait with purpose. This society seems to force us to move without hearing.

Now the Lord had said to Abram:

Get out of your country, from your family and from your father's house, to a land that I will show you. I will make you a great nation; I will bless you and make your name great. And you shall be a blessing. I will bless those who bless you, And I will curse him who curses you; And in you all the families of the earth shall be blessed" (Genesis 12:1-3).

THINGS YOU MUST DO

You must **listen** to the voice of God, "My sheep know my voice and another they will not follow." Knowing the voice of the shepherd takes time and frequent conversations. In the eastern culture the shepherd names each of his sheep and when he gathers them he calls them by name. If you were a sheep and you heard the shepherd every evening call you into the safe fold, or heard him speak over you while you were resting, or you heard him singing over you in the morning then his voice becomes a safe and familiar sound to your ears. The Bible says another voice the sheep will not follow, why, because they do not recognize the voice. The more you spend time with the good shepherd the more sure you become of his voice.

You must **hear the whole message** that the Lord is giving and **believe it.** Have you ever heard someone talking and before they have finished the message you ran off thinking you had the whole story? That happens when people are impatient and don't wait for the whole word from God. Sometimes He does not give you the entire message in one sitting. Sometimes He waits a few days to complete the thought he is sharing with you. What would happen if you were a messenger in the army and the captain of the army entrusted you with critical information that you needed to take to another regime. What if you ran off to take the message before the captain was finished giving it? The limited information that you obtained was not enough for the strategy to be fulfilled and it could cost your side a victory. Wait for the full message, make sure God is finished speaking before you move out.

Then you must begin to **walk** by faith because you will not see or understand perfectly what the Lord is showing you. We have some difficulty walking by faith because the land we grew up in has done a very good job of training us to walk by sight.

Faith is not seeing initially. As you walk by faith, eventually you will see the thing you have been hoping for. Faith has evidence and it has substance, however you won't see it at first. The first step is blind obedience. Although this faith walk is not easy, the benefits of walking by faith are more than can be numbered.

Look to Abraham your father, And to Sarah who bore you; For I called him alone,

And blessed him and increased him. For the LORD will comfort Zion,

He will comfort all her waste places; He will make her wilderness like Eden,

And her desert like the garden of the LORD; Joy and gladness will be found in it,

Thanksgiving and the voice of melody. Look to Abraham your father, and to Sarah who bore you; For I called him alone and blessed him and increased him (Isaiah 51:2-3).

Then there is the eye of faith. Abraham had it. He saw what was invisible and embraced it. You can see what is invisible. When you are still and waiting on God for the next instruction you can see in the realm of the spirit. God can show you things in dreams and visions. Dreams occur when you are asleep, but visions can materialize while you are awake. You can experience a vison while you are waiting for the traffic light to change or while you are sitting on your porch. The visions that you receive should be written down because not all dreams are for the moment nor should they all be taken literally. Some dreams and visions are symbolic. Ask God for the interpretation of the dream or the vision before you move on what you see. It is okay to seek out people that God uses to interpret dreams. Daniel was one that God used to interrupt dreams and so was Joseph. Joseph interpreted the dreams of the king and the interpretation saved the nation. If God trusts you with a dream or a vision please know that this is not just for you to keep but when you sense that this dream needs to be shared and interpreted for the benefit of the people who need to hear don't hold back. But this is the sight you receive in The Land of Faith.

I want you to remember also, that this journey and adventure is not a sprint, nor a jog, nor a forty yard dash this is a walk. The walk will require some energy and effort but not the kind required in a run. This is for the long haul. This walk will take you your life time. There is no hurry because everything you are to encounter on this journey will not be taken from you. You don't have to hurry and get the jump on someone else. What God has for you is for you. This walk allows for stopping at times to observe the beauty of your surroundings. Not everything in The Land of Faith is challenging. Sometimes you can rest and relax and look at the waterfalls and mountains and visit with others in the land, sit on the grass and enjoy a day of peace. Walking affords you the opportunity to experience things in the land that you might have missed if you are moving quickly.

7
No Turning Back

Then those who feared the LORD spoke to one another,
And the LORD listened and heard them;
So a book of remembrance was written
before Him For those who fear the LORD
And who meditate on His name. "They shall
be Mine," says the LORD of hosts,
"On the day that I make them My jewels.
And I will spare them
As a man spares his own son who serves him."
Then you shall again discern between
the righteous and the wicked,
Between one who serves God
And one who does not serve Him.
Malachi 3:16-18

THE KINGDOM OF GOD IS VOICE ACTIVATED, therefore you must talk about the new place you now reside in. The more you talk about where you are, the less you are likely to entertain the thoughts of going back.

One of the most powerful tools that are in your possession are words. The tongue is a powerful weapon on the earth. Your tongue can break yokes in the heart and in the mind. You need to be careful what you allow to come out of your mouth because life and death are in the power of the tongue. You have what you say, because God said so.

Listen, in this wonderful Land of Faith the deserts get pretty dry and the watering hole is nowhere in sight. The sun is beating down on your head and your feet are dragging in the dust. Just know this, your adversary the devil is going to be right there whispering in your ear, telling you all the reasons why you should have never come into this land in the first place. His goal is to get you to stop moving in the direction of the master's plan and turn around. What should you do when things are not working like you thought? What should you do when others seem to be getting where they need to go, and they talk to you and you feel a level of embarrassment or perhaps envy? Some of the people who started after you did are now moving farther ahead of you. At least this is what you perceive to be happening. But remember your eyes can deceive you.

What's up with that? In your mind you should have arrived at the specific destination by now. You think to yourself, why is the answer taking so long? Sometimes those who are single have a timeline on their mind. By this time, I will graduate from high school and then attend college or some form of higher education, then on to college. After college I plan to begin my career, meet the man or woman of my dreams and get married. We will purchase our first house and establish a beautiful life, maybe travel a little and then begin our family.

That sounds like a picturesque scenario. But how many know that things don't always work the way we plan. But no matter what events show up in your life either planned over time or suddenly you must remember that God is in control. Just because things are rough is not a reason to turn around and give up. People in the world have events that happen unexpectedly so why would you contemplate leaving The Land of Faith? Is it to make things happen faster? Not really not going to change things. I know that we have ideas in our minds as to how our lives should progress. When you graduate from high school you think that it will only be a matter of four years and I will graduate from college. I can't tell you how many people thought they would graduate in four years and it ended up being four and a half or maybe even five years and even in spite of the delay you still set another timeline. Words like next year I will be established in the profession that I want; and then by this time I will be married and by this time I will have children. By this time, I will retire and then travel with my spouse and live happily ever after. We tend to do that and have not really sought the Lord or asked Him about His timeline. Have we taken into consideration the wonderful plan that God has for us?

First, let me tell you that every time you receive promises from God, His words will come to pass. The issue is that when God tells you something, He rarely gives a timeline with it. We create our own timelines and set those in our minds. Most of us think our time is right now, immediately or at least very soon. But rarely does our timeline include the words, not now or later.

The primary thing you must do is learn how to wait without losing your hope, praise and your determination.

One thing you can learn from the children of Israel is what they did when they were in the wilderness. When things were not going right for the children of Israel they began to murmur and complain. They rehearsed the good things about being in Egypt. They said, "we wish we could have the leeks and the garlic." But what they neglected to say was that the leeks and the garlic came with a great price attached. Those vegetables were nothing compared to the whips and the lashes they received from the masters. They forgot about their children being taken into slavery at very young ages. They forgot about the hardships they endured. Leeks and garlic don't light a candle to the horrible things they were suffering as a people. That is why they cried out to God in the first place. They were severely oppressed as enslaved people.

This is the nature of people. They have what I call selective memory. The Bible says that Satan blinds the minds of people. II Corinthians 4:4 says, "They are caught between a rock and a hard place." When you get to those places in your walk here in The Land of Faith there are several things you should do. You must determine in your mind there will be no turning back!

Draw a line in your mind. Say to yourself that this line will not be crossed should you come to a place where you think turning around would be easier. You must get your eyes off the problem. Some problems loom very large in front of us. That mountain of bills, the phone calls from bill collectors, or that huge sickness that will not let go of a loved one. That co-worker that is constantly annoying us and giving us fits. That neighbor or the relative who needs so much, more than you have to give both physically and emotionally. Fill your mouth with praise and worship and if you can't seem to come up with a praise on your own, get your CD, phone, or get omline and type in praise and worship songs and let the device sing to you until you can join in. Eventually you will join in and the praises unto the Lord God will take over that thought of giving up or the feeling of turning back.

The enemy is constantly in there pitching with his perpetual dialogue. Perpetual dialogues are those thoughts that keep speaking to you day and night. They are negative in nature. They say things like "you never should have tried to follow God, look at what that has produced", or "you look stupid believing God for a miracle; you might as well give up."

Let's take a look at a Bible character whose name is Jeremiah in the book of Lamentations 3:19-27 (The Message)

> I'll never forget the trouble, the utter
>   lostness, the taste of ashes, the poison
>   I've swallowed.
> I remember it all—oh, how well
>   I remember—the feeling of
>   hitting the bottom.
> But there's one other thing I remember,
>   and remembering, I keep a grip on hope:
> GOD's loyal love couldn't have run out,
>   his merciful love couldn't have dried up.
> They're created new every morning.

How great your faithfulness!
I'm sticking with GOD (I say it over and
over). He's all I've got left.
GOD proves to be good to the man who
passionately waits, to the woman who
diligently seeks.
It's a good thing to quietly hope,
quietly hope for help from GOD.
It's a good thing when you're young
to stick it out through the hard times

Jeremiah's condition was a lot like ours. He had outward affliction and inward turmoil and these things pushed him to despair, however one thought crowded out the hopelessness that threatened to overwhelm him, "God's great love." Was this love limited? Would this love and compassion ever run out? This thought propelled him through exhausting and troubling times. Afflictions are only temporary, but God's love is from everlasting to everlasting. Jeremiah could place his affliction in proper perspective by remembering how it related to God's character and His covenant with His people. You have to say, "I won't go back, I won't look back!"

GO BACK TO WHAT?

Turn around? Not on your life, not a chance! He is all I have left. I'm going to stick to the plan, and if I have to stand still for a while then stand I will. But turning around is not an option.

You will then be able to engage the enemy with his perpetual dialogue. When he tells you that God has forgotten you for some dumb mistake you made. You have a comeback; John 10:3 says, "I have called you by name." If the Lord has called me by name, then He has me on His mind. This perpetual dialogue will try to sabotage your thoughts so that you will constantly wonder if the path you are on is worth it, or if it is the right one.

You mean to tell me that after all those valleys you have trudged through, and all the rivers you have waded in and all the mountains that you have come over, you are going to give up now? Not on your life! Listen, you have come too far to give up now. The promise is to you and to your children and to people that are a far off, those are people who haven't even been born yet. What about the people who have been watching you and have grabbed faith because of your testimony? What about those who were going to quit a long time ago back when they were facing a valley experience and they saw you pressing onward and strictly because of your determination they continued.

Don't think about your old friends and what a great time you all had. That thought process is a trick from the past. You know that right now those friends who have not turned to Jesus are as miserable as they can be. Some of them are in jail, in the grave, on their third and fourth spouse, have children who won't speak to them and they have a list of regrets as long as your arm. Don't think about your crazy days as though they were your best days. You know that those days were wrapped in fear, delusions, pain, anxiety, discontentment and wars within and without.

Start counting your blessings since the day you decided to make Jesus your choice. Sometimes you can start counting before you found Jesus. Come on count! First you have been given precious promises straight from the promise keeper. You have been surrounded by the angels of God who have been given charge over you to keep you. You have more prayers answered than you can remember. Take a trip down memory lane and recall the grace and the love of God shown you since you moved into The Land of Faith.

Come on praise the Lord!!

Just because you are facing something big now doesn't mean that God has diminished or become impotent. He is the same yesterday, today and forever more. God is not mad at you because you entertained the thought of turning around or going back. He sees you at a crossroad and you're choosing not to give up. He sees you under great stress but still holding on to your faith. He saw you when you put your Bible in the drawer and said I am through. He saw you when a blast from the past visited you and told you all the things that they are doing without the help of the Lord.

He also knows when He is going to bring you out of this. You see, because God knows the end from the beginning, He already sees you finishing the race and operating in a position of power and authority in the Kingdom of God. He sees you finishing and becoming a guide for others who decide to walk, live and abide in The Land of Faith.

Spend some time with Him not complaining but just receiving strength. It has been my observation that God does not give you extra, but usually He gives you enough to make the next step. Somehow you muster the strength to say "Hallelujah" then another one is right behind that one and then another and another until you are in full blown praise to the God of all flesh who is your good father.

Hear the word of the Lord from the psalmist:

I would have lost heart,
    unless I had believed
That I would see the goodness of the LORD
    In the land of the living.
Wait on the LORD;
    Be of good courage,
and He shall strengthen your heart;
    Wait, I say, on the LORD
(Psalms 27:13-14 NKJV).

So, you are not the first to feel like quitting or giving up but if you just wait on the Lord and encourage yourself, God is going to come and give you exactly what you need to make it through this hurdle.
    Turning Back? Not a chance!!

I've come
too far
to turn back
now!

Fulfilling the Mission In the Land

I will make you into a great nation and I will
bless you; I will make your name great, and you
will be a blessing. I will bless those who bless
you, and whosoever cures you will curse; and all
peoples on earth will be blessed through you.
Gen. 12:2-3

A LL OF US ARE PLACED or positioned where we can an
must impact these systems for the Kingdom of Go
Even though we are involved in these systems we must n
get caught in the snare of the system. Remember you li
in The Land of Faith. There must be light in the midd
of gross darkness.

While living in the land we are saturated with th
principles of faith so that we can interact with tho
living outside of The Land of Faith. That is our missic
on the earth. We are called to impact and invade th
earthly realm with the Kingdom principles. We have bee
positioned in these other systems for a specific purpos

Not to gain accolades from others, not to make money, or have our name in lights or on the lips of the masses. No, we are constantly on assignment for the Kingdom of God. Keep the main thing the main thing. In The Land of Faith God's purpose is the main thing. We cannot lose sight of the main thing.

We live in The Land of Faith to become salt and light in the world. We are governed by a different set of laws which come from the Word of God. We operate by another set of standards. We conduct our life affairs by a different set of guidelines. We dance to another song; it is the song of the spirit. We play, yes, we play but even when we play it is with the integrity of the land of our new birth. We are entertained by what governs every aspect of our life, which is in Christ Jesus. We are representatives of the Kingdom from which we have been born.

In Romans 8:5-9 we read;
For those who live according to the flesh set their minds on the things of the flesh, but those who live according to the Spirit, the things of the Spirit.
For to be carnally minded is death, but to be spiritually minded is life and peace.
Because the carnal mind is enmity against God; for it is not subject to the law of God, nor indeed can be.
So then, those who are in the flesh cannot please God. But you are not in the flesh but in the Spirit, if indeed the Spirit of God dwells in you. Now if anyone does not have the Spirit of Christ, he is not His.

The Land of Faith is a spiritual place. This is where the righteous are required to live if they want to please God. The word righteous means moral, honest, good, just, virtuous and upright. We can say that if you are carnally minded you cannot live in The Land of Faith. Living in the Land of Faith is life and peace. Walking in this land causes you to trust the one who led you here in the beginning. As citizens of the new Kingdom we have received the spirit of God; that we might know the things that are freely given to us by God. (I Corinthians 2:12)

The Land of Faith is a place that you had to leap into, but you can get out anytime you choose. There are no walls and no restraints in this land. The enemy of your soul is constantly trying to lure you out of this land. There are roadblocks and detours that will be placed at various junctures to derail and hinder you. Your soul must be made up and willing to comply with the perfect will of God. You have an obligation to speak to your soul and make it line up with God's plan and purpose for you. Proverbs says, "He that getteth wisdom loveth his soul: he that keepeth understanding shall find good."

Your soul is your will, emotions, intellect, and your desires. This soul of necessity must be corralled and tamed by the Holy Spirit. The one you yield strength to, is the one who will rule. You know what? It is essential to feed your soul the right things for your soul to develop the right attitude and produce the correct response to the wiles (*schemes*) of the devil. See you can purify your soul in obeying the truth through the spirit. I don't think I can say this enough, knowing the word of God and being filled with the word is paramount.

The flesh is kind of like the puppet on a string. The real puppet master can either be the spirit of Christ that dwells within you or your soul. The one who rules is the stronger of the two. The flesh just goes along for the ride. So, as many as are led by the Spirit of God they are the sons of God.

MISSIONS IN THE LAND (START HERE)

One mission will be to establish a pattern of living that resists the evil one's charm. There is a place you can get to where the enemy no longer has any success when he tempts you with going back. After you have suffered a while the Lord will establish you and settle you so that you will have no more desire to leave this beautiful land. Although trials will come, when you are in this precious land the Bible says:

> Beloved think it not strange concerning the fiery trials which is to try you, as though some strange thing happened unto you: But rejoice, since ye are partakers of Christ's sufferings: that, when his glory shall be revealed, ye may be glad also with exceeding joy (I Peter 4:12).

There was a TV series in 1983-1987[11] that I really liked, and it was called the A-Team. This group of men took on missions that were extremely difficult and many of them were missions that the U.S. government did not want to be connected to in any way. It usually dealt with foreign lands and people that had been kidnapped by a foreign power and the negotiations of the government failed. Many of their missions dealt with people that they had to rescue from the enemy or return something to its rightful owner. The A-Team had discussions in order to create strategies of how to successfully carry out the mission. Most of the time they only had a small window to pull off the task. They often went through character changes and several trial and errors. But at the end of every mission they managed to successfully complete the job. At the end of a successful completion the head of the group, whose name was Hannibal, would always say, "I love it when a plan comes together." I equate the A-Team missions to that of the missions of the believers in The Land of Faith.

SECOND MISSION

Our second mission is to rescue the lost. We cannot use the same strategy that we used yesterday on every mission. This is where the relationship with Jesus Christ is a must. You have to seek God and read His word and get the plan for each mission. There are so many people that need to be rescued. They all have the right time when their hearts will be tender, and their spirits are open to the message of freedom and deliverance. God will give you the right time. He will give you how to approach the one you are seeking. But know this that the enemy does not want you to accomplish any rescues. You will run into roadblocks. But keep the mission in the forefront of your mind. This one will be delivered. Zechariah 10:12 says, "And I will strengthen them in the Lord; and they shall walk up and down in His name, saith the Lord." Amen and Amen!!

When you have completed the task of "seek and rescue" you can stand up like Hannibal and say, "I love it when a plan comes together." Not your plan, but God's plan. In II Corinthians 5:11-21 it discusses that we as believers have been given the ministry of reconciliation that is one of our most important missions in The Land of Faith.

THIRD MISSION

Our third mission is invasion. We are to invade the seven spheres of influence and begin to influence them. In Pastor Sunday Adelaja's book *Church Shift*[12], he mentions seven spheres of influence;

1. Spiritual/Social
2. Government/politics
3. Business/economy
4. Education
5. Media
6. Culture/entertainment
7. Sports

The good thing about being in The Land of Faith is you can live one place and be in another.

We have been given information from the reconnaissance team that has gone before us. "Many are the afflictions of the righteous, but the Lord delivers them out of them ALL" (Psa. 34:19 KJV). Part of our reconnaissance team includes a name I think you might be familiar with. Let's start with Moses, he was on a mission and came to an impossible circumstance. However, God demonstrated to him that when God sends you on a mission; there is nothing that can stop you not even a large body of water i.e., Red Sea. God has the power to part it for you and you will walk through on dry land. In time of famine, Joseph is a witness that God will prepare you and provide for you in times of drought. In times of war, King David will testify that God delivered his enemies into his hands. In drought, God used a widow woman to provide for Elijah the prophet and both the prophet and the woman and her son were spared. Snakes?? The Apostle Paul showed us that even those things sent to kill you will not be victorious. He picked up some firewood and a venomous snake attached to his hand and bit him. He shook the snake into the fire and was not harmed. What about Hunger and temptations? Jesus is our example when in the wilderness he was hungry and thirsty and was tempted of the devil, but He did not succumb.

God has given us equipment and witnesses to navigate through this land and come out a winner every single time.

The Word of God tells us:

Finally, my brethren, be strong in the Lord and in the power of His might. Put on the whole armor of God, that you may be able to stand against the wiles of the devil. For we do not wrestle against flesh and blood, but against principalities, against powers, against the rulers of the darkness of this age, against spiritual hosts of wickedness in the heavenly places. Therefore take up the whole armor of God, that you may be able to withstand in the evil day, and having done all, to stand. Stand therefore, having girded your waist with truth, having put on the breastplate of righteousness, and having shod your feet with the preparation of the gospel of peace; above all, taking the shield of faith with which you will be able to quench all the fiery darts of the wicked one. And take the helmet of salvation, and the sword of the Spirit, which is the word of God; (Ephesians 6:10-17 KJV)

The more you talk to others about where you are, the less likely you are to entertain the thoughts of failure or going back.

In Malachi 3:16-18 it says:

Then those who feared the LORD spoke to one another, And the LORD listened and heard them; So a book of remembrance was written before Him For those who fear the LORD And who meditate on His name. "They shall be Mine," says the LORD of hosts, "On the day that I make them My jewels. And I will spare them as a man spares his own son who serves him." Then you shall again discern Between the righteous and the wicked, Between one who serves God and one who does not serve Him.

Praise and worship along with the Word of God will help you keep the main thing, the main thing. You will long to hear those precious words: "Well Done My Good and Faithful Servant!! Mission Accomplished!!!"

A Different Outcome

Women received their dead raised to life again.
Others were tortured, not accepting deliverance,
that they might obtain a better resurrection.
Still others had trial of mockings and scourgings,
yes, and of chains and imprisonment. They
were stoned, they were sawn in two, were
tempted, were slain with the sword.
Heb. 11:35-37

HEBREWS CHAPTER 11 IS COMMONLY KNOWN as the faith chapter of the Bible. In this passage you will find many examples of people who are highlighted for their faith. This is a fantastic chapter, and as I read it, I realized that there were those who had faith but did not receive the promise. Do you think that those who did not get delivered from the lions and those who did not get released from prison had less faith? Absolutely not! Their faith produced a different outcome.

I began writing this book about five years ago in 2016. I would start it then stop, then start again. This repetition continued for several months. As I neared the completion of this book, I felt like the Lord spoke to me and said that I was not ready to write the last chapter of this book. So, I put the book on the shelf and waited for the go sign. My husband, Bishop S. Michael Millben, and I had expectations of some things to happen soon and I thought the beginning of that phase was the material for the last chapter of this book or perhaps the beginning of a new book. I thought I had the plan all figured out. Then our lives were turned upside down in 2018. You know the kind of turn in life that leaves you standing or maybe laying with your mouth open and eyes blinking and barely able to breathe? You know the day when you feel gut punched?

That was the day when Michael and I were given the news that he had stage 4 pancreatic cancer and a possible two months life expectancy.

What??? How could that be? They must be mistaken. I've heard of doctors getting the information mixed up and giving the test results to the wrong person. Is that what's happened? Let me share some of our journey.

My husband and I were married 48 years. We met in Bible College and we were truly in love, yes, after all that time. Our love had taken us through some very trying times and some beautiful times. Through the birth of 3 beautiful children and the loss of one. Through no jobs and living in his grandmother's house and eating groceries that were given to us by a refuse collector to great jobs and home ownership. We were a typical family that loved God and had the call of pastoring on our lives. We served in the house of the Lord wherever we lived and trained our children to love and trust the Lord and to serve Him. We believed in divine healing and supernatural intervention in the affairs of our lives. God did amazing things for us and always made Himself known. His presence would fill our home to the point that at times people that came into our home could feel the Spirit of God. Michael and I had a deep relationship with the Lord. Many times I could sense the Lord calling me to prayer for a special reason. Those were times that trained me to hear and to know His voice. "My sheep hear my voice and I know them, and they follow." John 10:27

Over the years, Michael would tell me things that he heard while in prayer. We both were trained to hear and know the voice of the Lord. You never really know what you are being trained for, but the training will be used at different points in your spiritual walk. He heard God tell him to quit his corporate job and trust that He was leading him into fulltime ministry. That was a big jump for both of us because we were raised to believe that a man should work and take care of his family and fulltime ministry, in our minds, was kind of iffy. When Michael told me what he heard in prayer, he had a great job at Amway Corporation as an assistant personnel director. I began to pray as well so that I would not say anything disparaging. He was glad to have a wife that would pray with him and not against him. He didn't want to make a mistake and jeopardize our comfortable family life, but he was committed to follow hard after God. So, we both sought the Lord to make sure that it was Him. Not too long after that he received a call to come to Muncie, Indiana to become the pastor of Christ Temple Church.

I'm sharing some of this with you to let you know that we have followed God's leading throughout our lives. I'm not saying we have always heard correctly and done it right, but we sure tried. We also walked and lived in this land called faith and have seen many miracles. God had confirmed His word to us in many ways. He provided for us financially when things were looking bad and the Lord healed our bodies, the bodies of our children and many people that we had prayed for. We believed in the supernatural power of God.

So, when we heard, "stage 4 cancer" we just sat in the doctor's office and tried to breathe. The effort it took to breathe in those moments is difficult to articulate. We just sat, I'm not sure how long we sat. The doctor and his nurse didn't rush us out of the room, but they did tell us that he needed to begin treatment right away. We finally mustered enough strength to stand up and exit the office in total silence. The 30-minute drive home was in total silence. What is there to say? How can this be? Oh, but God was going to heal him. This was going to be another miracle that we will experience. We had plans for the next phase of our lives which included installing a pastor for the church we served for over thirty years and moving onto another level of ministry. My husband believed that a true minister of the gospel is a minister of the gospel until he or she dies, but it would take on a different look as time moved on. He could see himself pastoring pastors and helping develop men and women in leadership roles. Being a sounding board for ministers who needed a listening ear and who needed accountability. We were going to celebrate 50 years of marriage in 2 years. We were going to travel more and do more international ministry. We were going to become an intervention couple for missionaries who were having marital problems. We discovered that the divorce rate with missionary couples is increasing. Some of that is due to the fact that these couples give and give to others, but they have no one to pour into them. We saw the next phase including connecting with global programs that reaches out to just such couples.

Cancer?? No, that does not fit into the next phase at all! When we could finally catch our breathe, I called our children and asked them to come over, because we had some very important news to share with them. Let me pause right here and tell you that we have the best and the most supportive children anyone could ever ask for. Each showing support in their own way but standing with us during this most difficult time. When we met with the children my husband shared the news. They were silent and teary, but ready to help in any way possible. Asking, what can we do?

The next notification was to the church family. I will never forget the Sunday that my husband stood before the church and told them what was happening. First there was total silence. That seemed to be the reaction of everyone who heard. Then there were prayers being prayed right then and there. The saints knew where our help was going to come from. Remember I have said throughout this book that The Land of Faith is not heaven. This time was proof of that. In heaven there are no tears and no pain; we were experiencing both. We were hurting, baffled, and stunned. Then our children sprang into action. They first wanted to know what was their dad's desire. He said, "No Chemo". Okay, then we needed an alternative to chemo.

Our oldest daughter Kizmin began researching and looking up alternatives to traditional cancer treatment. She found two treatment centers in Mexico, but the problem is that alternative treatments are not covered by insurance. One center's cost was $52,000 for a 21-day treatment plan. That was out of the question. The next center was the same amount of time in Mexico, but the cost was over $21,000. Upon hearing the difference in cost, I questioned the level of care. I was told that they offered the same treatments just less opulence. The cost was still more than we had. But when you live in The Land of Faith you see things before they manifest. We didn't know how but we knew that if this was God's will then he would make a way. Some people are very private about situations like this, but our philosophy is, when people of God are made aware of what you are dealing with, they will pray more specifically. I know that the prayers of the righteous avails much.

Kizmin started a fundraising effort and explained what we were facing, and the support came in. The generosity of pastors, family members, friends, and formers associates was overwhelming. We actually had friends drive from out of the state to support us. The outpouring of love from the pastors in our city made both of us cry when they came and prayed for him and filled our laps with tokens of love to help us go. I really don't think my husband knew how much he was loved and respected until this happened. I think we need to verbalize to others how much we appreciate things they do in the moment. You never know how your words can lift the other person up. Don't think that pastors don't need lifting and encouraging. He or she does. A kind word can go a long way. People are not short on criticisms, but they are short on words of affirmation.

We not only needed money for the treatment, but we needed money to stay in a hotel, for round trip airline tickets to Mexico, to eat and to pay for transportation for three weeks. Lord have mercy! God did it, the money came from many sources. Our church leaders stepped up and took care of the church while we were gone. That was love in action.

We thought we were ready to fly to Tijuana, Mexico but before we could leave, my husband got real sick. His eyes were very yellow, and his skin had a yellow tint to it. We went to the hospital and they admitted him and told us that he had a blockage in the bile duct in his liver which was causing him to become jaundiced. They said unless they performed surgery to open that duct, he would not be able to fly to Mexico. They performed the procedure and in a few days his eyes were white and his skin back to normal. Michael Millben was a general of the faith. He was talking faith all along the way. He would even encourage me when I felt down. Listen, in The Land of Faith you will have moments that doubt will try to creep in, especially if you look at the circumstances with your natural eyes. Your eyes will give you a different picture than the Word of God. Trust God's Word.

Finally we were cleared to fly, and we prepared to leave. I thank God that our daughters insisted on accompanying us on this journey. Kizmin came for the first 10 days and Brittany came for the second 10 days. They sacrificed and left their families to come and help their dad and I. I love them so much for that. God also sends you aide in The Land of Faith.

The center was very nice, and the people had such a positive attitude that you couldn't help but be encouraged.

While in Mexico I began to write every evening sharing with the people about the day and the progress. God actually gave me a song every morning while we were there. They were songs whose message was exactly what I needed for the day. The Word of God and the songs from the spirit encouraged me to believe no matter what my eyes saw. Some days Michael was completely drained from 7 hours of treatment and all he wanted to do when we got back to the hotel was lay down and rest. It was nice to have Kizmin and Brittany there for company. We played games and read quite a bit because other than one or two channels, the television stations were all in Spanish. We found that the area where our hotel was seemed pretty safe, so we ventured out in the evenings. We found a huge pharmacy that sold everything, including food. So, we went there to get various drinks that we had a taste for. It was nice to walk and see the sights and get some fresh air.

When we arrived in Mexico, my husband had two lesions, one on his pancreas and one on his liver. At the end of week three the lesion on his pancreas had disappeared. What???? Thank you Jesus! When the doctor gave us the news that the tumor was completely gone. We sat for just a few seconds trying to let the news sink in. I asked the doctor to repeat what he had just said. He said that the tumor on his liver looked like a pimple that had popped. That there was only a ring where the tumor had been. What?? Immediately I shouted, "Thank you Jesus!"

After leaving the office, I ran down two flights of stairs praising God. I ran outside down the street and back. The joy that filled my heart was unexplainable. I knew God was moving. But the doctor also said that they did not get the entire tumor on his liver. They wanted us to stay longer, but we were out of money, and could not stay any longer. We took home various medicines and herbs that he had been taking there, so we could continue the treatment as best we could in the states. We were living in The Land of Faith, so we believed that God could and would remove the tumor on the liver as well.

We came home excited and full of faith. Then he began to get sick again and experiencing severe back pain. We returned to the hospital again and they suggested that we begin hospice. What?? Within two weeks of returning home, a new tumor appeared on his pancreas and the liver tumor had increased in size.

Hospice to me meant that we were giving up. No!! Absolutely not! There is no need for Hospice because God is going to raise him up, right? It was strongly suggested that we have Hospice come in to assist me with his care. They also said that if he had any hospital needs, he could bypass going to the emergency room. That part of it was a good thing, so a Hospice plan was implemented. I kept thinking, okay God any day now I know you are going to come through and raise him up. I believe you.

The weeks passed and the pain increased to the point that he could hardly bear, so they placed a pain pump in his back to help lessen the pain. Pancreatic cancer is a beast. I watched this mighty man of God drop about 70 pounds. I kept saying, nothing I see will move me from my belief. I believe God will heal his body and what a testimony he is going to have.

Living in The Land of Faith means that you get an audience with the King of Kings and you can express your heart's desire. He will hear you and will answer, but the answer isn't always "Yes". Some answers are "Wait" and some are "No". So, wait a minute, I thought you were living in The Land of Faith? I thought that in The Land of Faith you have access to God and that He hears and answers prayers? Yes, that is correct. Until this experience, I thought that once you moved into The Land of Faith all the answers were Yes. But I have come to realize that all the answers are not yes. Sometimes you will get a No! What do you do when the answer is No?

The true fruit of Faith is continuing to love and trust God even when you get a "No". Let me tell you this part is not easy at all. Trusting that God has made the right decision to say "No" means that you will have to reach way back into your knowledge of Him and pull from a place of experience. You know deep in your soul that God is sovereign. What He does is right and good even when we don't understand or agree.

I am sitting here today on the other side of "No". Do I turn around and give up, and stop walking with God? Do I leave this Land of Faith and go back to ......What??? I heard something this morning that has inspired me to continue no matter what. I heard a preacher say that when you get a "No" from God, He has also given you grace to handle the "No". God gives you the grace to balance out the heavy "No". He did that for the Apostle Paul, when He told him that His grace was sufficient.

The "No" we received from God when we asked for healing for my husband, felt like a slap in the face with a heavy hand. I could not believe that God did not raise him up. I could see if he was an ungodly person, a mean person, a hypocrite, a liar, a thief, or some other unsavory type person, but this was a good man, a wonderful father, an excellent husband, and a great pastor. He was so smart yet humble. He was not the type to boast of his accomplishments even though he had many. He really liked riding motorcycles. He was an out of the box thinker and wasn't afraid to move in a different direction if God prompted him to do so.

The fruit of faith in this land that we call home produces trust and more faith. I will trust in the Lord until I die, why? Because "no" does not mean God is mad at us or that He hates us. We got that idea from the land of our nativity. Spoiled children cannot accept a "no" from their parents. They act like that is not a word in their vocabulary. They believe that the mere fact that they are in this family should ensure that a "yes" always comes from my parent's lips A spoiled child cannot be denied their heart's desire or they will throw a fit. We've all seen those children in the store who cannot tolerate their parents saying "no". They scream and holler until the parents acquiesces and gives the child what they want. Caving in is just the adult's way of preventing a scene. God will not be pushed into a corner like that

That reminds me of a scripture in the Bible in Psalms 106:13-15:

> They soon forgot His works;
> They did not wait for His counsel,
> But lusted exceedingly in the wilderness,
> And tested God in the desert.
> And He gave them their request,
> But sent leanness into their soul.

This scripture is talking about the children of Israel, but they sound a lot like the people of God today. We beg God and beg God until He gives us what we ask for and then it turns out to be the worst thing in the long run. A"no" is necessary at times to develop a stronger bond and a deeper trust in our heavenly Father.

My dearest husband called all his children and grandchildren together one evening and prayed over them and blessed them. He even made them laugh. He spoke over the congregation the last time he ministered to them and left them with the word, "Everything will be Alright".

He and I spent time together and he told me to finish strong, stay current on forgiveness and to remember that many of the things we think are important are really nothing. In the last days of his life he prayed a lot and basked in the presence of the Lord. The spirit of God would come in the room and flow over him like a cool breeze. On Sunday evening, December 9, the praying ceased because the final answer had come. "No" was God's final answer to the question I and many other people had been asking for 6 months. That evening he closed his eyes for the last time in this life.

I often reflect on what I could have done differently, and I have concluded that no human being could have done anything to reverse "No". This was a set time; we just didn't know it.

So, I continue to walk in this Land of Faith. I point people to the only One that has the power to say "Yes," "Wait" or "No". With the yes comes **gratefulness**, with the wait comes **patience** and with the no comes **grace**. The Land of Faith has an expanse beyond comprehension and experiences that will be worth writing about.

It is my hope and prayer that this book has inspired you to leap into The Land of Faith and never leave.

Having
therefore
obtained help
of God
I continue
unto this day
(Acts 26:22)

NOTES

Chapter 1: Land of Faith

1. "Hope." *Merriam-Webster.com Dictionary*, Merriam-Webster, https://www.merriam-webster.com/dictionary/hope. Accessed 13 Apr. 2021.

2. May, Sandra. "What Was the Space Shuttle?" *NASA*, 7 Aug. 7. 2017, https://www.nasa.gov/audience/forstudents/k-4/stories/nasa-knows/what-is-the-space-shuttle-k4.html. Accessed 10 July 2019.

3. Wilerson, D., Sherrill, E. & Sherrill, J., *The Cross and the Switchblade*. Chosen Books, 2008.

4. "Nihilism." *Merriam-Webster.com Dictionary*, Merriam-Webster, https://www.merriam-webster.com/dictionary/nihilism. Accessed 13 Apr. 2021.

5. "Faith." *Merriam-Webster.com Dictionary*, Merriam-Webster, https://www.merriam-webster.com/dictionary/faith. Accessed 13 Apr. 2021.

Chapter 4: Topography of the Land of Faith

6. "Topography." *Merriam-Webster.com Dictionary*, Merriam-Webster, https://www.merriam-webster.com/dictionary/topography. Accessed 13 Apr. 2021.

7. "Rivers." National Geographic, https://www.nationalgeo-

graphic.com/environment/article/rivers. Accessed 14 April. 2021.

8. Ruden, Sarah. "The God of Running Water." *Laphams Quarterly*, Vol. XI, No. 3, Summer 2018. https://www.laphamsquarterly.org/water/god-running-water. Accessed 14 April. 2021.

Chapter 5: Faith that Moves God

9. "Humility." Merriam-Webster.com Dictionary, Merriam-Webster, https://www.merriam-webster.com/dictionary/humility. Accessed 14 Apr. 2021.

Chapter 6: We Walk

10. "How the Eye Works as a Camera." American Mascular Degeneration Foundation, https://www.macular.org/eye-camera. Accessed 14, 2021.

Chapter 8: Fulfilling the Mession in the Land

11. *A-Team,* created by Frank Lupo & Stephen J. Cannell. Universal Televisons, 1983-1987.

12. Adelaja, Sunday. *Church Shift.* Charisma Media, 2008.

ABOUT THE AUTHOR

Denise Millben co-pastored Christ Temple Global Ministries with her husband S. Michael Millben for over thirty years. She is currently the Apostle and overseer of several ministries. She is a teacher, a Bible scholar, author, counselor & international speaker. Denise has traveled the world declaring the gospel of Jesus Christ.

She is the founder of the Bridge-to-Life organization, which is dedicated to bringing K-12 education, clean water and sustainability to countless third-world countries where these facilities are scarce. Denise authored *Two Silver Trumpets*, a book focusing on couples in ministry and her newest book, *I Miss Poppy*, a book helping children through grief.

Denise is a mother to her three children and eight grandchildren. She continues to minister the gospel around the country and abroad. She resides in central Indiana.

To know more about Denise, follower her on Facebook at (Denise Millben).

To contact Denise Millben
P.O. Box 1945
Muncie, IN 47308
email: copastordenise@aol.com

ALSO AVAILABLE FROM DENISE MILLBEN

Ministers of the Gospel give of themselves to their congregations, but trying to maintain the balance in marriage when both spouses are in ministry can be challenging. *Two Silver Trumpets* focuses on the struggles married couples in ministry have and how to maintain a balance in their marriage.

I Miss Poppy is Denise's first published children's book. It focuses on helping children cope with grief and manage their emotions when someone they love passes away. It is a great book to help any adult recognize some of the emotions behind the actions of a child.

Made in the USA
Monee, IL
27 July 2021